YOU CAN WIN *BIG* IN SMALL CLAIMS COURT

YOU CAN WIN *BIG* IN SMALL CLAIMS COURT

Judge JAMES E. MORRIS

RAWSON, WADE PUBLISHERS, INC.
NEW YORK

Library of Congress Cataloging in Publication Data

Morris, James E.
You can win big in small claims court.

Includes index.
1. Small claims courts—United States.   I. Title.
KF8769.M67   347.73′28   81–1499
ISBN 0–89256–177–7   347.3074   AACR2
    0-89256-202-1 (Pbk.)

Copyright © 1981 by James E. Morris
All rights reserved
Published simultaneously in Canada by
McClelland and Stewart, Ltd.
Composition by American–Stratford Graphic Services, Inc.
Brattleboro, Vermont
Manufactured in the United States of America by
R. R. Donnelley & Sons Co.,
Crawfordsville, Indiana

Designed by Jacques Chazaud

First Edition

For Kim and Debbie
Who make the sun shine every day of the year

For Mom and Dad
Who equipped me for life's journey

For Bill and Pat
Who helped me put it all together

Acknowledgments

Once the idea of writing a book for the general public on small claims was presented to my friends, their support and encouragement were inspiring.

THANKS:

To my brothers, Stephen P. Morris and Richard D. Morris; to William J. Goldman, William J. Gedale, Charlotte Nuciola, William Brongo, and Richard Friedfertig;

To my special friends who have helped me in so many ways more than they know; the court clerks in the town of Brighton, Josephine D'Ambrosia and Virginia Bergan; to Brighton Associate Judge John Ark for helping assist me with my court duties; to Ellen DeClerk, the Small Claims Court chief clerk for the city of Rochester, New York;

To Judge Harold L. Galloway, chief administrative judge for the city of Rochester, New York who has given me the opportunity to be of service since 1977 to the city of Rochester City Court;

To retired Justice Thomas F. Hanna, the most dignified and wisest judge whom I have served with or appeared before in my legal career. By his standards he has set high goals for any attorneys or judges to attempt to achieve;

To Ruth Jelline Morris for the preliminary editorial work she has done; she is a true professional in every sense of the word. To Lisa Healy, my editor, who has provided not only support, but also the intellectual challenge necessary to write this book; I am deeply indebted to her. And to Eleanor Rawson for putting faith in me and recognizing the public's desire to learn more about righting the wrongs;

To Richard Pine, my agent, who has encouraged me greatly from our first contact;

To the National Center for State Courts, Williamsburg, Virginia, for permitting me to draw upon published material, particularly *Small Claims Court: A National Examination* by John C. Ruhnka and Steven Weller, as technical background information that has confirmed my belief from experience as a Small Claims Court judge;

And especially to my personal secretary, Carol Russo, whose faithfulness and loyalty to me in this project have gone far beyond the call of duty;

And to all the people who have appeared in Small Claims Court.

CONTENTS

PART ONE—Step-by-Step Procedures

CHAPTER I—What Can Small Claims Court
    Do for You?   *3*

CHAPTER II—Understanding Small Claims Court
    . . . Nothing to Be Afraid Of   *8*

CHAPTER III—You *Can* Win if You Bring a Claim to
    Small Claims Court   *13*
  Do you have a valid claim?   *13*
  Finding the proper court   *19*
  Your meeting with the clerk   *21*
  What to do if your opponent calls   *25*
  Doing your homework   *26*
  The role of the judge and what to expect in the
    courtroom   *28*
  Use of arbitrators instead of judges   *33*
  Use of lawyers in Small Claims Court   *34*

CHAPTER IV—You *Can* Win if You Are Sued   *36*
  Receiving the notice   *36*
  Preparing the defense   *37*
  Your appearance in court   *38*
  Cases in which other persons may be responsible   *40*

CHAPTER V—After You Have Completed the
    Presentation   *42*
  The decision   *42*
  Collecting the award   *44*

If you lose 46
Appeals are discouraged 46

PART TWO—The Cases

CHAPTER VI—Contracts; Breach of Obligations to Perform 51
Separation Agreements 52
  Alimony arrears 53
Promissory Notes 56
Failure to Fulfill Contract 57
  Misrepresented tour service 58
  Services Contracted for but Not Performed 61
  Return of deposit from painter 62

CHAPTER VII—Your Insurance Company's Failure to Pay You as the Insured 65
Claims Against Homeowner's or Renter's Insurance Company 66
  Failure to pay claim for flood damage in home 66
Claims Against Your Health Insurance 70
  Reimbursement for medical expenses 71
Claims Against Your Automobile Insurance Company 74
  Dispute with claimant's insurance company over amount to repair 75

CHAPTER VIII—Landlord-Tenant Claims 78
Claims Against Landlords 79
  Return of security deposit 81
  Return of security deposit; defense, improper notice by tenant 83
Claims Against Tenants 87
  Landlord claim against tenant for damage 88

CHAPTER IX—Defective Goods and Merchandise 91
Defective beauty product 92
Defective floor covering 94

Defective jewelry	*96*
Request refund of money for defective automobile	*98*
Defective Product—Good-faith Respondent	*101*
Defective silverware	*102*
Defective Product Resulting in Consequential Damages	*104*
Defective refrigerator and spoiled food	*105*
Defective Product—Improper Installation	*108*
Inoperable burglar alarm	*109*
CHAPTER X—Services Performed	*112*
Improper Services Performed	*113*
Improper dress alteration	*114*
Improper dyeing of leather boots	*115*
Materials not paid for; counterclaim, improper painting and wallpapering services performed	*118*
Improper, Unnecessary, and Unauthorized Repairs	*122*
Automobile repairs billed, but not performed	*123*
Improper lawn mower repairs	*125*
Improper repair to clothes washer	*126*
Services Rendered Properly, but Unpaid	*130*
Unpaid professional services—dentist	*131*
CHAPTER XI—Negligence	*135*
Dealing with Negligence—Automobile accident	*136*
Collision damage—question of liability	*139*
Collision damage—question of amount entitled to	*140*
Negligence by Workmen	
Damage to automobile from paint overspray	*142*
Negligence While Performing Service	*147*
Damage in car wash	*147*
Damage to Your Goods by Negligence While in Possession and Control of Others	*149*
Improper dry-cleaning services—damage to fabric	*150*
Auto damage in parking lot	*155*

CHAPTER XII—Heartbreak Cases 159
   Personal Property Not Returned 160
   Return Cost of One Half of Furniture 162
      Money due and owing based on promise to pay 164

CHAPTER XIII—Claims in which a Child Is a Party 167
   Actions by Infants 168
      Replace clothing damaged from dog bite 168
      Failure to pay infant for services rendered—money owed paper carrier 170
   Claims Against Infants 173

CHAPTER XIV—Claims Against Your Local Government or Governmental Agency 174
   Damage for Sewage Backup 177
   Negligence on Behalf of School District—Improper Supervision 180

CHAPTER XV—Intentional Damage and Missing Goods—Lost or Stolen 184
   Claims for Injury or Damage Suffered from Intentional Acts 185
      Damage to snowmobile 185
   Missing Goods 188
      Clothing missing from laundromat 189
      Missing tire 192

SUMMARY 195

APPENDIX A: Small Claims Court Flow Chart 196
APPENDIX B: Table of Variations of Small Claims Courts by State 197
GLOSSARY OF TERMS 209
INDEX 215

PART ONE

Step-by-Step Procedures

CHAPTER

I

What Can Small Claims Court Do for You?

WARNING: If it hasn't happened to you yet, the odds are pretty high that it will soon!

- You are stopped in traffic waiting for the red light to change. An inattentive motorist slams your car in the rear. After contacting his insurance company, you are told that only 70 percent of your claim will be paid because you were partially at fault. Upset, but not wanting to bother to contact a lawyer or waste any more time, you reluctantly agree to accept a check for 70 percent of what you feel is due.
- After you've spent two days on your hands and knees scrubbing the floor of your apartment so that you can obtain your security deposit back, your landlord sends an inspector. Several days, or even weeks later, you are notified of deductions for many items and receive a check for your security deposit less $150 for "general service charges." Understandably angry and frustrated, you try to contact your landlord but he won't return your phone calls, so you let the matter slide.
- A washing machine repairman refuses to leave until you give him a check; only two days later, your washing ma-

chine exhibits the same symptoms and the repairman ignores your pleas. Another repairman fixes the machine for a fraction of the original bill, indicating that nothing was done by the earlier repairman. You know that you have been exploited, but you'd rather let it slide and say, "Well, I'll just never call him again."
- How many times have you purchased a product you found was not as the salesman told you once you got it home? When you tried to get your money back, he said, "Sorry." Has anyone ever performed a service for you such as painting or cleaning which hasn't been done properly, thus cheating you of some of the money you paid in advance? Has someone failed to pay you for services you performed for them and you felt angry and manipulated?

These cases are typical of events that happen literally thousands of times each day in our country. How many people realize that there is a remedy available, a procedure by which in a very brief period of time *you* can have the last word in each of the above matters? *You* do not have to be taken advantage of by the impersonal insurance company, the rich landlord who is probably retaining from everyone a bit more security than he should, and the repairman who just moves on to perform improper services for another one of your neighbors, as well as all of the others whom you feel have taken you.

I am sure you can think of dozens of times when you felt that you were overcharged, or an improper service was performed for you after you paid, or that someone didn't keep to his or her end of the bargain and you lost money as a result of it.

This book introduces you to the procedure to "right the wrongs": Small Claims Court. These courts exist in various forms throughout the United States. They provide a forum for you to bring a claim against a person, company, or even a governmental body for varying sums up to $5,000, depending on the area. In each instance, the procedure is simple and uncomplicated. A lawyer is not required, and in fact in most Small Claims Courts lawyers are discouraged from attending. The judge is often friendly and wishes to hear the issues between the parties, seeking the truth in a manner that does not stick to any strict rules of evidence.

A major advantage of Small Claims Court is its speed. In fact, once you file a claim, a hearing is often held within thirty days. The costs of filing a claim are nominal and the judges usually are fair and compassionate.

These are the courts of the people—those who are rich, poor, uneducated, college graduates, senior citizens, students, those on all levels. From the time you file a claim in Small Claims Court you are treated equally, regardless of your station in life. Rules are the same for all. Informality prevails.

In the pages that follow, you will learn how to use these courts in *step-by-step procedures,* explained in plain and clear language. Much of the information given in this book is a straight view from the bench as seen through my years of experience hearing hundreds of cases in Small Claims Court. Although the names in the cases have been changed, the incidents and the impressions they made on me as a judge are passed on to you without change. The rationale of a judge as to why he decided a certain way will be helpful to you in developing your case and proving it before the court.

Although you may be tempted to go directly to the case area of this book, don't! In order to gain full knowledge and feeling for Small Claims Court—its procedures, cases, and people—you should read this book from cover to cover. Although the facts in each case area may differ, a full reading will place your problem in perspective and teach you how to deal with your particular case.

Once you have learned how to bring an action in Small Claims Court with confidence, you can tell the person who has wronged you, "If you don't send the money I am entitled to, I will take you to Small Claims Court." No longer will you walk away from the person who took advantage of you and think to yourself, "Well, I guess I just learned a lesson," or think that nothing can be done. Even in claims of small amounts of money —of five, ten, or twenty dollars—you can right the wrong by using Small Claims Court. Your threat will not be an empty one.

This book tells you how to determine whether your claim is a valid one that has merit and will make a good action. You will learn in a simple, direct manner how to document your claim and how to prepare it, and how to bring out the winning parts of your case in the best possible light. You will learn how to act in court in front of a judge and how to address your opponent. The inner workings of the court will be revealed, just as if you were taking a guided tour, so that no surprises will await you.

You will also learn from reading the case section of this book that not all claims are valid. It will help you determine whether your claim is of good merit. You will also be told how to defend a claim that is not valid.

A complete reading and understanding of the book may also help prevent potential claims. You will know to write down agreements between parties to avoid misunderstandings; you will know to request, receive, and keep all of your receipts and canceled checks; you will also know the importance of obtaining witnesses to an event; you will know when it is important to obtain expert opinion—all of this and more to help you prevent an appearance in Small Claims Court. In the event a claim should result, your preparation will help guarantee your success.

Small Claims Courts in general are used only for those matters that involve a claim against a person or corporation for an amount of money owed. In addition to resolving such disputes on a legal level, often a judge will try to persuade those involved to resolve their disputes on a human level as well, in order to resume a business or personal relationship. The heartbreak cases are those in which there was a close relationship between the disputants that subsequently deteriorated. Sometimes the only way that ex-lovers or ex-fiancées are able to communicate the final termination of a relationship is in a

What Can Small Claims Court Do for You?

lawsuit brought in Small Claims Court dividing their property. Cases such as these, which are almost unresolvable on the personal level, are described later in this book.

There is nothing to fear in appearing in Small Claims Court, since judges are often very sympathetic to the plight of beleaguered citizens and have heard many cases such as yours before. Sometimes a decision is given from the bench immediately after the case is heard. Sometimes a judge wants to think about a case and will not decide it until a few days later, at which time you will receive notification in the mail. Although the emphasis in this book is on bringing a claim, a section is devoted to the position of the person against whom a claim has been filed. In the event a claim is without merit, or for a discussion of the method of settling a claim, the respondent's point of view is considered.

After reading this book you will no longer have to take the word of the insurance adjuster as final when he tells you that you were wrong in an accident even though you knew you were right. You will never again have to listen to your landlord say, "I'm sorry, but I'm deducting $150 from your security deposit for general cleaning." The repairman who did the imperfect job in your house will not get away with doing this to you. In a mild but confident manner you can say, "I'll see you in Small Claims Court!"

CHAPTER

II

Understanding Small Claims Court... Nothing to Be Afraid Of

SIMPLE, EFFICIENT, SPEEDY, low-cost, fair, and effective are the words that best describe this court procedure in which you can "right the wrongs" without being represented by an attorney.

The procedure used in Small Claims Courts began in the early part of the twentieth century in certain limited areas so that disputes between neighbors could be heard by a judge in a simplified procedure without lengthy lawsuits, delays, and the use of confusing legal jargon.

Small Claims Courts now exist throughout our country. Although certain rules and maximum limits of damages may vary slightly from State to State (see Appendix B), there is a common thread of justice that prevails.

Many people are reluctant to use any court procedure because of fear of the unknown. In any unfamiliar situation, anyone feels anxious, nervous, and tense because of lack of knowledge and experience. However, you should be aware that Small Claims Courts are set up for persons like yourself, and are run by people who are human beings much like you, from secretary to clerk to court attendant to the judge, who is there for the

Understanding Small Claims Court

purpose of listening. The judge wishes to understand the issues and understand the feelings of the people before him so that he may make what he believes to be a fair decision.

Small Claims Courts have set up procedures that are just waiting for you to come in with valid claims so that their purpose may be met—to hear disputes that require a remedy of an award of money damages to the claimant from the person being sued, the respondent.

Some states limit a claim to less than $500, whereas others have progressively, with inflation, raised their limits to nearly $5,000. The average maximum limit in the United States is between $750 and $1,000. No claim is too small for Small Claims Court, as the cases discussed later will illustrate. A judge will spend as much time dealing with a claim for $20 as he will for a claim for a much larger amount. He realizes it is important for the people before his court that he devote his patience and attention to each claim equally.

Judges who hear small claims sit in the local courts, the lower courts, the "courts of the people." In suburban and rural areas, they may be called justices of the peace or town judges. In urban areas, the courts may be called city courts, civil courts, or municipal courts. One day, a local court judge may hear traffic cases such as those involving speeding, improper passing, running red lights, or parking tickets; another day, he or she may hear criminal cases involving petty crimes or civil cases such as tenant evictions and many other common, everyday problems. As a general rule, Small Claims Court judges are not serving in courts that hear serious felony cases such as murders or bank robberies, or those involving large money judgments, such as million-dollar accident cases. Generally, they also do not hear appeals from other court decisions.

The judges of the Small Claims Courts are in touch with the people. These judges experience daily the frailties of human beings and their feelings, as well as the nature and basis of their claims. When a case is brought before a lower-court judge he or she wishes to learn all of the facts in an informal setting in order to arrive at a fair decision.

There are many kinds of cases that can be brought before a Small Claims Court. Among these are: compelling people to pay money agreed in contracts, including separation agreements and promissory notes; getting compensation for services you performed for which you were not paid; suing your insurance company when it failed to pay you for claims on your homeowner's, medical, or automobile insurance; suing for return of your security deposit, or landlords suing tenants for rent due and damage; getting compensation for defective merchandise and any resulting damages you suffer; bringing an action against a person who performed poor or unnecessary repair services for you; property damage claims in automobile accident cases; broken personal relationships; lawsuits by children for work done; claims against municipalities and governmental agencies; compensation for intentional damage to you or your property; and actions for missing goods that were entrusted to another person. The list could go on and on, since there are no limitations to the controversies human beings get themselves into.

As you look through the Contents or the Index of this book, you will see that nearly one hundred situations and types of cases are discussed. These are the most common. Among them you are sure to find those that are closely related to the claim *you* are considering.

In most states, small claims must be heard within thirty days from the time you file. Memories are fresh. Financial positions of both the claimant and the respondent are current. The merchant against whom you bring a claim is still in business. And generally, hostilities will have a chance to defuse quickly, instead of building up over many months or even years. The procedure is simple, effective, and to the point. It is not clouded by legal technicalities or bogged down in difficult jargon, procedure, or red tape.

In contrast, a case that is litigated through normal court

procedure with attorneys could take two or three years before a court date is reached. By then, of course, memories fade, witnesses and those involved often have moved or changed their financial status or may even have died.

The costs of Small Claims Court are minimal. Filing fees range from $2.00 to $10, plus the cost of serving notice through certified registered mail upon the person against whom a claim is brought. Once there is an award, if it is in your favor, you recover these costs from the other party. No matter what the size of the claim, the costs remain the same.

The most important factor in maintaining low costs in Small Claims Court is that *no attorney or lawyer is required.* In fact, judges do not see attorneys as being advantageous to a claimant. Many lawyers are aware of this and encourage their clients with small claims to go to court without them. An attorney's fee would diminish the value of your award, since, generally, legal fees may not be added to an award.

If one person comes to court with an attorney and the other without one, the judge, in many cases, instinctively takes the role of advocate for the person without an attorney.

If an award of money is made to you and it is not paid voluntarily, a civil enforcement officer such as a constable, marshal, or sheriff will, upon your request, obtain papers from the court enabling him or her to collect your money for you. This is not a police procedure, but purely a civil procedure for collection of judgments, as you will learn in Chapter V.

Corporations generally are not permitted to use these courts of the people to collect their business debts. The theory is that if a business chose the advantages of being incorporated in order to limit liability from certain claims, it should not be permitted to use this simplified procedure to collect small claims. They can, however, be sued as respondents, and once sued, may bring a counterclaim against the person bringing an action.

Jury trials are discouraged in Small Claims Court, as they are contrary to the idea of a simplified procedure. In most jurisdictions, once you file a small claim you waive or give up any right to a jury trial. If a jury trial is demanded, a costly court bond must be posted and the case is transferred to a regular court and treated as a more complex civil matter.

Appeals are unusual. The judge's decision may be appealed, but the procedure is awkward and costly. Each state has certain restrictions on appeals. In some areas, judges refer the cases to arbitrators whose decision is binding. No further appeal may then be made. It is very important, therefore, to make your best presentation in the best possible light at the time the claim is originally heard.

In the chapters that follow, you will learn step by step how a judge views a case from its preparation to its presentation. Your understanding will be increased by reading about actual cases in which people have attempted to right wrongs and have succeeded.

CHAPTER

III

You *Can* Win if You Bring a Claim to Small Claims Court

YOU CAN WIN if you bring a claim to Small Claims Court. But first, you must show in a logical, step-by-step manner that you suffered a monetary loss as a result of another person's wrongful actions and that the person who wronged you is legally responsible for your loss. It is not enough merely to come into court and state that the person whom you sued *may* have caused you to lose money or be injured. You must clearly state the specific actions that caused the loss and also prove the *actual* amount of the loss.

DO YOU HAVE A VALID CLAIM?

In order to determine whether you have a valid claim, you must first determine that you have been "wronged." Ask yourself these questions: Has another person:

- Failed to fulfill a contract, so that you sustained a financial loss?

- Done something that was improper or negligent, resulting in injury or damage to you or your property?
- Failed to do something that resulted in damage to you or to your property?
- Taken advantage of you in a way that resulted in a financial loss?

You must next be able to answer "yes" to the most important questions:

Did the other person cause the loss to me?

Is there some basis in law to have a court award the money damages?

Determining the validity of a claim is simple in some cases; more difficult in others. The following are examples of cases in which the claims may be valid:

Has another person failed to fulfill a contract so that you sustained a financial loss?

Your landlord failed to return your security deposit when you were ready to move out of your apartment. You feel you deserve to have the security deposit returned; you bring a claim against your landlord. In this case, the landlord failed to fulfill the contract with you to return the security deposit at the end of the term of the lease. He caused you to lose the amount of the security deposit that was not returned. The basis in law is that agreement you made together. You fulfilled your end of the contract by keeping to the terms of the lease and by keeping the property in good order, but the landlord failed to fulfill the contract by failing to return the security deposit. You, therefore, have determined that you have a valid claim.

Has another person done something that was improper or negligent, resulting in injury or damage to you or your property?

Your legally parked car is hit from the rear by a careless driver. You have suffered collision damage. The operator of the other vehicle was negligent. The other person caused the loss to you by careless driving. Basic law places the blame and liability upon him. You may bring a claim in Small Claims Court.

Has another person failed to do something that resulted in damage to you or to your property?

Another example of a valid claim is a claim for additional damages that you suffered as a result of improper work (consequential damages) such as the work of a repairman who advised you that all you needed to fix your refrigerator was a replacement of a worn belt. After replacing the belt and charging you the sum of $27, he assures you that the refrigerator will work. You later find that he placed the wrong-sized belt on the compressor, which resulted in $86 worth of food being destroyed. You may then bring action not only for the cost of the improper repair, but also for the food damages as the result of this improper repair.

Has another person taken advantage of you in a way that resulted in a financial loss?

You perform certain services for another person at an agreed rate of $10 per hour and you work for five hours; you are owed the sum of $50. You are not paid. The other person's failure to pay you resulted in damage to you. You may compute your loss at $50 and bring a claim in Small Claims Court. The failure of the person to pay you has resulted in your loss. You should be awarded the full amount of $50.

Similarly, if you have a promissory note that entitles you to money over a course of time and you have not been paid, the failure of the respondent to pay you is cause to sue in Small Claims Court.

Did the other person cause a loss to me?

In each of these cases, you have determined that the person you are suing actually caused your loss. You must also determine if there is an actual monetary value you can place on your loss. Sometimes it is simple, as in the above examples, to assess damages. On the other hand, if the damage you have suffered is abstract or speculative, such as aggravation or inconvenience, you cannot place financial value on it. You have not suffered an actual financial loss, and would, therefore, not be able to proceed in Small Claims Court.

Is there some basis in law to have a court award the money damages?

Once you have determined that you have been wronged, that another person whom you can name specifically has wronged you, and that you can place a value on the loss, then you must be certain that there is some basis in law for your claim.

Small claims consist of disputes in which people have a general knowledge of their rights, be it through contract or through familiarity with the common types of cases set forth in this book.

Is there a question as to who is liable?

There are cases in which you have been wronged by a person whom you don't know, but you attempt to place liability on a person whom you do have a relationship with. For example, if you are a landlord and rent to a tenant, and a third person comes on the property without the invitation of the tenant and causes damage, you may try to collect from the tenant. If the tenant caused the damage or the person was on the property with the tenant's knowledge and consent and in fact caused the damage with his knowledge and consent, then the tenant would be liable. However, in most cases, damage was not caused with the tenant's knowledge or consent and, therefore, there would be no liability by the tenant to the landlord.

In cases in which you have any question of liability, the clerk of the Small Claims Court may be able to assist you. He or she may ask you to provide written documents such as estimates, receipts, bills, or other letters between you and the person whom

You Can Win if You Bring a Claim to Small Claims Court

you wish to sue. These documents could show necessary proof of your claim and thus eliminate the question of liability. If a doubt remains you may also be directed by the clerk to consult with an attorney to determine whether or not the matter would be worth pursuing. There are different rules in each state.

Timing

A rule that further defines which cases may be heard in Small Claims Courts sets time limits on commencement of suits. This is called the statute of limitations. As long as your claim is brought promptly, as a general rule you will not have to be concerned about being barred by any time limitations. The statute of limitations in most states is at least two years on most claims.

If you are having a dispute with someone that develops into a valid claim, you should make some demand upon the other person or company to see if they will voluntarily pay the amount you are owed. Do not waste time waiting for a response. If within a few days you have not received a satisfactory response, you should take steps to file your claim in Small Claims Court.

Some companies are in business only for a short period of time. If they are able to delay your filing a claim long enough by promising and not delivering, by the time you get around to filing your claim they will be out of business and your ability to collect will be close to zero.

In Chapter XI, you will learn about the negligence of SPL Contractors, an out-of-town company spray-painting a bridge. For six months Gus and Cindy Stone listened to promises that a check for damages was in the mail. By the time they got around to bringing an action in Small Claims Court, the company had moved out of state and beyond the reach of Small Claims Court jurisdiction.

Another advantage of filing promptly is that memories fade with delay, and witnesses become unavailable.

Other Factors to Consider

You should also make certain that your action is not barred by other factors, such as the fact that you might have signed a release of any liability against the person whom you are suing. For example, a person recently brought an action in Small Claims Court to collect damages in an automobile accident. His total claim amounted to $500. The insurance company sent him a check for $150. On the reverse side of the check was a general acknowledgment that endorsement of the check would constitute payment of all liability against the party represented by the insurance company. In addition to that, the insurance company enclosed with the check a letter indicating that acceptance of the $150 would result in payment in full of the claim.

By cashing the check and accepting it as it was tendered, the insured party was barred from bringing any future action. The person did bring a claim in Small Claims Court, and the judge indicated the claimant could not collect because of his having signed the release. It is, therefore, important for you to determine that there is no defense such as time limitations or signed releases that could bar you from collecting. You will not have a case if you sue a person for an unpaid debt and the person produces a receipt showing that the debt was paid. All of these factors are important in determining whether or not you have a valid claim.

CHECKLIST FOR DETERMINING IF YOU HAVE A VALID CLAIM

- Has another person failed to fulfill a contract so that you sustained a financial loss?
- Has another person done something that was improper or negligent, resulting in injury or damage to you or your property?
- Has another person failed to do something that resulted in damage to you or your property?

- Has another person taken advantage of you in a way that resulted in a financial loss?
- Can you prove that the other person caused a loss to you?
- Is there some basis in law to have a court award money damages?
- Is there any question of liability?
- Is your action barred by any legal defense such as a release or statute of limitations?

When Small Claims Court Is Not the Answer

If you are involved in a dispute with another person in which the relief of money damages is not appropriate, you should seek an alternative forum. For instance, if you are having trouble with your neighbor about cutting a hedge, or if you are asking that another person stop a certain activity, you should determine if a center for dispute settlement is available in your community. Such centers often settle disputes informally by using mediators and arbitrators. You do not need an attorney to seek relief in this manner. Once you have contacted the Small Claims Court clerk and have learned your case may not be appropriate for that court, you may ask the clerk if a community dispute center is available. Usually you will find these centers listed in the phone book under "Community Dispute Center" or "Arbitration Center."

FINDING THE PROPER COURT

After you have concluded that you have a valid claim, you must then find the proper Small Claims Court in which to file. The rules giving power to the Small Claims Court vary in each state as to the maximum amount of money for which you can sue and as to the specific Municipal Court in which you can bring the claim. This is called *monetary jurisdiction* and *geo-*

graphical jurisdiction. The appendix in this book will tell you which rules apply in your state. There is only one Small Claims Court in your locale that can hear your specific case.

The simplest way to find out where you should bring your claim is to telephone the local Small Claims Court. It may be listed in the phone book as a Municipal Court, City Court, District Court, Justice of the Peace Court, or Town or Village Court and will be found with the general listings of your city, county, town, or village government agencies. When you place a call to the local court, the person you reach will be a clerk of the court who can answer your specific questions. The clerk of the court is your most important source of help in small claims. Unlike other courts, Small Claims Courts routinely deal with the general public. The clerks are accustomed to answering inquiries and most are very happy to talk with you. Don't feel that a phone call is an imposition. One important role of the employees of the court is to aid you in the process of filing and preparing your case.

When you call the Small Claims Court in your area, you should first tell the clerk that you would like to file a claim. Then ask what the maximum amount of money is that you can sue for in Small Claims Court. Tell the clerk where you reside and where the respondent does business and resides. The clerk will then tell you whether you can file in that local Small Claims Court. If you have called the wrong court, you will be advised as to the proper court. In some states, you must bring an action in the court of the area where the respondent works or lives, even though this may not be the most convenient for you. In some courts there are other rules, such as that either party lives within the county of the court's jurisdiction. These rules can be complex, but by furnishing basic information to your local Small Claims Court clerk, you will be properly directed.

Once you've found the appropriate court, ask the clerk which documents will be required for the type of claim you intend to file; how much money is required as a filing fee; and what form the money should take. Fees generally range from $2.00 to $10. You may also want to ask for directions for getting to the court; the hours you can file a claim; and if there is parking nearby.

CHECKLIST FOR FINDING THE PROPER COURT

- Look up phone number of your local Small Claims Court.
- Call your local court clerk.
- Advise the clerk what town, city, or village you and the respondent each live or work in.
- Tell the clerk the amount for which you wish to sue and the general nature of the claim.
- Ask which documents are needed.
- Determine the hours and days you can file a claim.
- Find out the filing fee and whether it should be in cash or by check.
- Find out the location of the court and parking.
- Be brief and to the point (the clerk does not want to know all the details of your claim on the telephone).
- Prepare for your meeting with the clerk.

YOUR MEETING WITH THE CLERK

After you have determined the proper court in which to file your valid claim, you should prepare for the first personal contact you will have with the Small Claims Court by obtaining all of the documents required for presentation of your claim. Many clerks will screen a case first so that you will not be wasting your time in filing a claim without any evidence to back it up. You should obtain any estimates of damage or repair, accident reports, letters, contracts, promissory notes, leases, canceled checks, or other items that will be convincing documentation of your claim.

You should also obtain the full legal name of the person you are going to sue. If you do know the party personally, look at the documents you are going to present for the official name of the person. If you are going to sue a woman, you may not sue her as Mrs. John Smith, but must sue her in her full name, such as Susan Smith. First names should be used, not initials. If you are suing a business, you must determine if it is a corporation or a person doing business under a business name. You can determine this by checking any documents you may have with the respondent's name. If you don't have any documents, you could check the phone book, a city directory, or even call the respondent to obtain the legal name.

In many states it is required that a business file with the municipal or county clerk's office. By checking with a clerk in that office, you may obtain the proper legal name of the company you are suing. If it is a corporation, you should sue it as the corporation, such as ABC Corp. or ABC, Inc. If, on the other hand, it is a business such as Handy Dandy Service, you should find out who the person is who actually owns and runs Handy Dandy Service. Assume you have found that the name of the person is John Jones. In this case, you sue using both names on one notice, such as John Jones d/b/a (doing business as) Handy Dandy Service.

It is also important that you have the proper legal address of the person whom you are suing so that you and the clerk can fill out the claim form and obtain the necessary service of notice upon the respondent. The address should be current, should include the Zip Code, and should not be a post-office box. The address is also required to determine if the court can exercise jurisdiction over the respondent.

Determine next the type of case you have, whether it is a breach of contract, insurance company's "failure to pay" case, landlord-tenant, defective merchandise or services, negligence, action against a municipality, or a case of intentional damage or missing goods. Think of a way to describe in twenty-five words or less why the respondent owes you money. This summary

You Can *Win if You Bring a Claim to Small Claims Court* 23

will assist the clerk in helping you. You will be told what documents to bring to court to prove your case.

You should know the precise amount of damage you have suffered so that you can advise the clerk of the exact amount of money for which you are suing. Be sure to include any amount of sales tax that would be added to the amount of goods or services. If you are in doubt as to the amount, look at the documents you have. In addition to your actual loss, you may collect consequential damages, as you will learn later in the case section (see *Tillman* v. *Bill's Appliance Center* in Chapter IX). Also included in the amount of your claim are actual expenses directly resulting from the loss. Attorney's fees, however, are not included.

Bring the necessary filing fee with you. You may also want to bring your calendar or appointment book so that when the clerk tells you of a date for trial, you will immediately know whether you will be available.

You are now ready for your meeting with the clerk. Remember to be organized and brief. Do not tell the clerk all of your woes regarding your loss. He or she is only interested in the most pertinent details. You will be given a form to fill out (or the clerk may fill it out for you) whereon you must classify the type of action you have. For instance, if you want your security deposit back, your case will be considered a landlord-tenant case. On the form you will have to provide the following information:

- Your name and address and those of the person you are suing.
- The amount of money being claimed.
- A brief (twenty-five-word) explanation of why you are owed money by the respondent.
- Your signature and the date.

After you have filed this form, a notice will be sent to the respondent, which will state that he or she is being sued; what he or she is being sued for; the date and place of the trial; and any additional directions. This notice will be sent to the respondent by one of three methods: (1) personal service by a sheriff, marshal, or other authorized person; (2) registered mail with return receipt, which is the most common method; or (3) first-class mail. This varies in different jurisdictions. Registered mail with return receipt is better than first class since it assures the receipt of the notice by the respondent. Even if the respondent refuses to pick up his certified mail at the post office, it is still deemed to be sufficient service by most courts.

The clerk will give you a receipt for your filing, which will include the name of the case, a docket or case number, and the date of the court appearance. Keep this document, as you may have to present it or refer to it when you appear in court. Some courts refer to cases by the calendar or docket number instead of the name.

While you are meeting with the clerk, it would be beneficial for you to ask if you could go into the courtroom where the claim will be heard. This will familiarize you with the setting and will help you to avoid unnecessary anxieties. If the court is in session, you can sit in on a few cases and observe other people presenting claims.

If the clerk tells you that you do not have a valid claim, or that you have some weakness in your case and refers you to your attorney for consultation, don't become upset or annoyed. The clerk is attempting to be helpful by keeping you from wasting your time.

CHECKLIST FOR YOUR MEETING WITH THE CLERK

- Short verbal summary of your case.
- Any papers used in the contact that resulted in the claim, including estimates, accident reports, letters, contracts.
- Proper name of respondent.
- Proper work or home address of respondent (not post-office box).

- Know the amount you seek.
- Be sure the court date the clerk gives you is okay.
- Be brief and to the point.
- Filing fees—usually cash is required.

WHAT TO DO IF YOUR OPPONENT CALLS

Once you have paid the clerk the small filing fee and signed the necessary claim form, the wheels are put into motion notifying the respondent that you are going to see him or her in court. He or she really knows now that you mean business. In many cases, the mere filing of a small claim and the respondent's receipt of a notice may result in quick settlement of the matter. If the case is clear-cut, the respondent may not want to go to court. He or she may contact you and immediately make arrangements to pay the debt.

If the respondent does contact you to pay the debt, you may accept it before the court date. Be sure that you include in any settlement the filing fee that you advanced. You should then promptly notify the clerk of the settlement.

If, in fact, you only have a promise that the respondent will pay, you should tell the respondent that he or she must show up in court and state the settlement on the record in front of the judge.

Unless you have been paid the agreed-to amount prior to court, both parties should appear in court and report the settlement to the judge when called on. That way if either of you does not keep your agreement, the matter may either be rescheduled without filing a new claim, or an automatic judgment may be granted against the party not adhering to the settlement.

CHECKLIST FOR WHAT TO DO IF YOUR OPPONENT CALLS

- Tell him or her why you brought action.
- Do not consent to adjournment.

- You may discuss settlement.
- Keep your cool.
- If you settle and it is not paid before Court, both must appear.
- If it is paid, claimant should notify clerk before court date.

Sometimes, a person who is sued will offer a portion of the claim, even though he or she does not believe it is owed. You may then discuss a compromise with the other party and enter into an agreement that settles the claim and removes all uncertainties of a courtroom win or loss. In fact, a prehearing settlement is the same as winning, because you have obtained the satisfaction of a positive response from the respondent. It was only through your taking the initiative and filing a valid claim with the clerk of Small Claims Court that you jarred the respondent into acting and acknowledging the debt.

DOING YOUR HOMEWORK

You will have from two to four weeks from the time of filing until the court date to complete your preparation. During this time you should outline the manner in which you will present the case to the judge. You should obtain any necessary documents to persuade the judge that your claim is accurate. In some jurisdictions, you can present statements of witnesses without the witnesses being present in court. You should check with the clerk to see if a statement from a witness would be satisfactory. Often a court will not accept a statement from an absent witness because an absent witness cannot be cross-examined by the other party. However, certain statements, such as those concerning estimates of repair, are usually permitted by state law to be considered by the judge and given whatever weight he or she determines.

If there are any witnesses who are important in your case

(people who were aware of the incident or relationship that is at issue), you should ask them to come to court. It is important that you understand that the number of witnesses you present does not enhance your claim. The presentation of a claim is strengthened by the quality of the evidence, not the quantity. A judge does not decide the case on the basis of which side presents the most witnesses.

If you require a witness's appearance in court and that person will not come voluntarily, you may ask the clerk to issue a subpoena. This document is an order of the court that requires a witness to appear at the time a case is heard. You may have to advance certain mileage costs to the person you subpoena. This will vary from state to state. If you require a document or records to present to court, you may ask the clerk to issue a *subpoena duces tecum.* This document will require that the person who has custody of the records or documents deliver the items to the Court before you present your case. Once again, the clerk will assist you in the proper procedure.

If it would simplify or clarify the presentation of your claim, you may show any appropriate diagrams or charts. For example, if an automobile accident is the issue, a large diagram of the intersection or area where the accident occurred would clarify the situation. Any photographs showing what you are trying to describe in words are usually helpful. These photographs should be clearly focused and should show good contrast. Those that need explanation are usually unsatisfactory. You may also present any actual physical evidence at issue. For instance, if defective merchandise was purchased, you may wish to bring it into court to show the judge exactly what was wrong with it.

You will have a better understanding of how to present your type of case after you read the cases detailed later in this book.

A general rule is that your presentation should run no more than fifteen minutes. It will have to be brief, to the point, and well prepared. This does not mean you should write out your presentation, as that often results in a delivery that is awkward and unnatural. But you might want to jot down a few key words to remind you of items you wish to present and their proper sequence. Practice the presentation of your claim either to yourself in front of a mirror or to a friend. Have your friend ask you certain questions to try to anticipate what the judge or other party may ask. Many valid cases have been lost because of inadequate preparation. It is important for you to practice your presentation so that you will not leave out any key factors that support your claim.

THE ROLE OF THE JUDGE AND WHAT TO EXPECT IN THE COURTROOM

You have prepared your case and are ready for your day in court to tell it to the judge. Be sure to arrive at the courtroom promptly. It would even be beneficial to be early. As you arrive, you will see many other people waiting to have their claims heard. Small claims cases are usually scheduled several at a time. Once you enter the courtroom, you will notice that there is a stenographer, a clerk, and a court attendant. A stenographer records everything that is said in the court. If a court clerk is present, he or she is available to assist you and the judge in handling evidence. The court attendant is present to direct you to the proper court, to tell you where to stand, and generally to keep order in the court. Although judges' styles vary from individual to individual, there are primarily two types of judges in Small Claims Courts. Some are passive; they listen to all of the evidence presented, take notes, and later render a decision. Others are aggressive and aid you in the presentation of your case by asking key questions to move you along. These judges get at the core of the issue very quickly. If you are shy or quiet or leave something out, most judges ask questions to help determine what happened to the missing parts. Their questions often serve to remind you to include an item you have left out.

You Can Win if You Bring a Claim to Small Claims Court 29

Most men and women who are judges are very interested in small claims hearings. They believe that this is the court closest to the people and that justice can be done in a simple and informal manner. They do not adhere to strict rules of evidence, as this often means getting involved in a boondoggle of legalese. The judge, who is experienced in what is acceptable evidence, will often consider that which in another court is normally unacceptable and will discard it if it isn't valid. Judges are used to hearing people's stories and are quite good at discerning the truth. On occasion, you may meet a judge who is impatient or gives the impression of not wishing to be in the courtroom. In this case, it is very important that you are polite, brief, and to the point. Follow the directions of the judge. If he or she tells you to move on to the next point, do so. If you are told, "I have heard enough," do not say anything further.

After you are seated in the courtroom, the judge will enter and all will stand. You will then be asked to be seated and a calendar or schedule of cases will be called to determine who is present. When your name is called, you should answer, "Ready."

If your opponent is not present, you will be asked to tell the judge about your case, and you must establish sufficient written or oral evidence to justify an award in your favor. This is called the establishing of a *prima facie* case. This means that you have given the judge enough information (when not questioned by your opponent) to prove your case. This enables the judge to determine if the amount of money you are suing for is recoverable under law. You will be awarded a default judgment if the respondent does not appear and you can establish a *prima facie* case. In addition to the amount you seek, the judgment will include the court costs you have paid. You may also be awarded interest. This is up to the discretion of the judge and is based upon two factors: the time that has elapsed since the claim arose and the amount of the award. It is computed at a legal rate of interest, which differs from state to state. It is not necessarily the same rate of interest you may receive in a regular bank account. Certain expenses are not recoverable, such as your transportation costs to the courthouse; baby-sitting; and other incidental charges in the prosecution of your claim.

Respondents fail to appear for several reasons. Perhaps the respondent was never served with a summons. You will have to come back on another court date and make arrangements with the clerk for another attempt at service of the notice on the respondent. Or perhaps the respondent realizes that the money was, in fact, owed and just wants to make it more difficult for you to collect. Or maybe the respondent is afraid to appear in court. Once you are granted a default judgment, you can contact the clerk of the court for advice on how you can collect the money (this is discussed in detail in Chapter V).

If the respondent does appear and answers "Ready" when your case is called, you will be asked to step forward and present your claim. If more than one judge is hearing claims that day, you may be assigned to another courtroom for presentation of your claim.

When you are first called to present your claim, you will be administered an oath affirming that the statements you will make are true. It is very important that you present only truthful claims and make statements of fact you believe to be true. Not only can a judge usually see through falsehoods or half truths, but also it is very easy to get tripped up. If you exaggerate or lie, the judge may disregard all of the truthful things you have said because your credibility at that point is diminished.

You will present your claim first by telling briefly what your claim is about, how it arose, and why you believe the respondent owes you a specific sum of money. You will document your claim with any physical evidence or documents you have prepared. If you have estimates, bills, letters, checks, or any other documents necessary for the court to view, you should have a

You Can Win if You Bring a Claim to Small Claims Court 31

copy for the respondent to examine. It might be best to make a copy for yourself to keep, as you give the judge the original. You may then have any witnesses testify on your behalf. The judge may ask you questions, which you should answer directly and succinctly.

The respondent will then have an opportunity to respond to your claim. You should permit him or her to respond without interruption. The judge will often ask questions of the respondent as well. During the hearing, you will have an opportunity to ask specific questions of the respondent or of anyone who testifies. The time for asking questions of your opponent is after your opponent has completed his or her presentation. You should, however, look to the judge for direction as to when you may ask questions, as each judge will conduct the hearing in his or her own way.

When you are presenting your case, it is important that you are cordial to the judge and court officials, polite to the respondent, and do not lose your temper. Small Claims Court cases can be very emotional and personal in nature. It is important, therefore, to keep your cool during the entire procedure. If you don't, it disturbs the judge's concentration and may impair your own credibility.

While in court, do not act like an attorney. You should present yourself as you really are. Often people come into court and attempt to use legal words that not only are unimpressive to the judge but that often are misused. Leave any legal language you may know at the courthouse door and pick it up on the way out.

Often the judge will attempt to settle the case before hearing all of the evidence. The judge also may ask for a certain action of the respondent, rather than a monetary settlement. For instance, if a repairman did improper work, rather than awarding the claimant a money judgment, the judge might ask the repairman if he would go back and do the work properly. If the claimant agrees, that might settle the case (unless the redoing of the work is also unsatisfactory; then an award of money would be made as an alternative). Although this happens rarely, it is a possibility in Small Claims Court. The judge can be flexible in an attempt to achieve justice in each case.

After the judge has heard both sides, he or she may render a decision from the bench and attempt to work out a payment schedule. Often, however, the judge will reserve judgment to think about the facts of the case; you will be notified of the result within several days.

When you have presented a claim successfully and been awarded an amount of money in Small Claims Court, this results in a judgment. A later section of this book will discuss the enforcement of the judgment.

CHECKLIST FOR PRESENTING A CLAIM

- Find proper court (see Checklist).
- Call Small Claims Court clerk for information.
- Gather all necessary documents of your claim.
- File claim at proper court (see Checklist).
- Visit court before your date to become familiar with surroundings.
- Notify your witnesses to appear.
- Appear on time (even early)—very important.
- Answer "Ready" when called.
- Present facts in *logical* order.
- Do not use any legal language you may know.
- Be calm and courteous.
- Present your witnesses to support your claim.
- Give the judge any documents to support your claim (and have a copy ready for your opponent).
- Ask questions of your opponent.
- Ask questions of opposing witnesses.
- The judge may ask you questions—respond directly.

- If you win, call the clerk about ten days later if you have not been paid.

USE OF ARBITRATORS INSTEAD OF JUDGES

In a few limited areas, Small Claims Court litigants will have the choice between going to an arbitrator or a judge. An arbitrator is an attorney who is sworn in by the judge to hear Small Claims Court cases only. The arbitrator may serve in that capacity one day a week, one day a month, or even less. This system was developed in New York City as an alternative to a judge hearing a case. If, for example, the Small Claims Court calendar is congested with many cases, the clerk will announce that there are arbitrators ready to hear the cases, should the parties agree. If you do choose arbitration, you are waiving any right to an appeal of the decision. The case is heard in a more informal atmosphere than the courtroom, usually in a jury waiting room or conference room.

Arbitrators are qualified people carefully selected by the judges who appoint them. They act more informally than a judge. Arbitrators try to settle the claims by working out a compromise between the parties more frequently than a judge might. The choice between having a judge or arbitrator hear your case is one that can be made at the time of the hearing if this option is available to you. If you have any questions, the clerk will be very glad to help you.

In some other localities, there is a limited use of lawyers, instead of judges, to hear Small Claims Court cases. These lawyers are called referees. They wear robes and act as if they were full-time judges. Their appointments are usually on a daily basis and they are assigned to help avoid backlogs. If your case is heard either by an arbitrator or a referee, you should proceed as you would if a judge were hearing the case.

USE OF LAWYERS IN SMALL CLAIMS COURT

Small Claims Court is intended to be a court of the people where technical rules of evidence are not used. Judges universally prefer that people do not present cases with attorneys. Often, when one party is represented by an attorney, the judge will take the role of the other party to protect his rights and may even bend over backward unintentionally. Most judges believe an attorney's representation of one party is detrimental in a Small Claims Court case. Attorneys tend to lengthen the trial process and undermine the intent of a Small Claims Court. Often, if an attorney appears, the judge will ask him or her to step back and merely observe the case instead of participating.

Having an attorney is advantageous to a party if the matter has already been decided in another court. This would be the case if you were involved in a divorce that set a certain division of property, and later on your ex-spouse brings an action to have you reimburse him or her for property arising out of the same relationship. The attorney would be able to explain that this had already been decided and present the necessary papers. Also, an attorney might be helpful in the type of case in which he or she had represented you (not necessarily in court) in dealing with the transaction. For example, you purchased a house and while represented by an attorney you negotiated for certain items such as a refrigerator and stove to go with the house. If, when you opened the front door, the items were gone, your attorney might be helpful in explaining the background to the court. An attorney may serve a useful role in Small Claims Court if there are certain unique rules of law that should be pointed out to the court.

If both parties are represented by attorneys, they may be able to work out a settlement merely by discussing the matter. Otherwise, if both parties are represented, the judge may transfer the case to a regular part of the court wherein all the proper rules of evidence are followed.

It is generally agreed by judges, lawyers, and people who appear in Small Claims Court that the appearance of an attorney does not better your position. As a general rule, you should appear without one.

CHAPTER

IV

You *Can* Win if You Are Sued

RECEIVING THE NOTICE

YOUR LETTER CARRIER arrives with a piece of mail and asks you to sign the return receipt. Your curiosity mounts as you sign the card and are handed an envelope. Now you see the return address of the local Small Claims Court. Your heart drops. For the first time, you are being sued in Small Claims Court. As you open the envelope, you see a simple notice, which informs you that someone is claiming you owe him or her a specified amount of money. The notice further informs you of the specific date and time you must appear in court to tell your side of the story.

While the emphasis in this book is on helping you bring a valid claim, it is also important that you be able to defend yourself against an invalid claim. Even though studies show that most people who bring cases to Small Claims Court are successful in receiving the award they seek, some claims are without merit. If you are being wrongly sued and you present your defense well, you'll probably be successful. This chapter deals with the defense claim.

It is very important that you take your court notice seriously. If you put it on your desk or dresser and forget about it, a judgment for the amount asked, plus court costs, will be taken against you automatically (presuming that the claimant's case is valid). Service of the Small Claims Court notice is usually made by registered mail, return receipt requested. If you had not been at home or at your place of business when the letter carrier arrived, you would have been notified to go to the post office to accept the notice. You should go there promptly, accept the mail, and sign for the letter so that you can start preparing your defense.

If you refuse to pick up the notice, the court may believe you intend to ignore it and may enter a judgment or award against you.

Other forms of service of the notice include the use of first-class mail, with the presumption that if the letter is not returned, service of the notice is complete; or a notice may be served upon you personally by a court officer or other person designated to serve papers. Regardless of the manner in which you are served, you will see that the notice includes the name of the party suing you and that person's address, the reason for the action being brought, the amount sought by the suing party, and the court date on which you must appear.

There are several ways for you to respond to the notice. If you believe that you do in fact owe the money to the person suing you, you should contact the claimant and attempt to settle the claim. If you do reach a settlement, you should notify the court clerk, who will tell you the proper procedure to follow.

PREPARING THE DEFENSE

If you are unable to reach a settlement, you should begin to prepare your defense immediately. In order to do this properly, find out as much as you can about the claimant's action against you. If you can reach the claimant by telephone, ask him or her why the claim was filed. Also, by learning what specific evidence the claimant has to document his or her claim, you can better prepare your defense. Just as the claimant has obtained all necessary documents and witnesses in preparing his or her claim, you should gather any documents regarding the transaction between you. You may obtain photographs, charts, diagrams, canceled checks, receipts, or other items of pertinent physical evidence. You should notify any witnesses that you would like to testify on your behalf. If they will not do it voluntarily, you should request the court clerk to issue orders (subpoenas) directing the appearance of the witnesses.

If you have a claim against the claimant in the same transaction or another transaction, you may raise that claim in court at the time you appear and, in fact, you will be acting as a person bringing a claim. This is called a counterclaim. You should contact the clerk for the proper procedure in advance, but usually, you will be able to raise the issue orally in court without the necessity of filing any papers. Before the case actually begins, you should advise the judge and the claimants that you wish to make a counterclaim against the claimant, the nature of the claim, and the amount. Your preparation should be the same as any person filing a claim (as discussed in the previous chapter).

YOUR APPEARANCE IN COURT

You must appear in court on the correct date and at the right time. If you do not, the award will almost automatically be made against you for the amount sought. It is important to pay careful attention to the facts the claimant presents while outlining his or her claim against you. You will have a chance to ask questions of the person bringing the claim and of his or her witnesses. You should present your facts and documents in a logical, chronological order. Do not say, "I object," or raise any other legal points. That is for the judge. Also, do not use any legal language you may know. Be certain to show any documents or other physical evidence that support your defense. If the judge asks you questions, answer them directly. You should bring extra copies of all documents you intend to present to the judge so that you can give them to the other party.

In Small Claims Court the judge will be eager to hear your response to the facts the claimant has claimed as the basis for the suit against you. If you have a valid defense you should tell your side of the story specifically, point by point.

If the claim against you is for improper workmanship or defective merchandise and you believe that you should redo the improper work or exchange the defective merchandise, you should advise the judge.

A TV repairman appeared as a defendant in a claim in which the claimant was suing for the total value of a $150 television set. The claimant asserted that he took the set in for repair, paid $12, brought the TV home, and found that it did not work properly. Instead of going to another repair shop, he went to Small Claims Court, where he said that the respondent's improper repairs had ruined the television. The respondent repairman told the judge he would like another opportunity to repair the set to the satisfaction of the claimant at no charge. The judge agreed, and several weeks later was advised by the parties that the respondent had completed the repairs satisfactorily. The claimant didn't really want the $150, but merely wanted his television in good working order. In this case, the respondent spoke up and indicated he was willing to redo the work. The judge was able to adjourn the case for several weeks to give him an opportunity to remedy the defect in his workmanship. If you are sued, therefore, and would like an opportunity to remedy the situation in question, the judge may give you that chance. This is discussed in Chapter IX, dealing with the good-faith respondent.

CASES IN WHICH OTHER PERSONS MAY BE RESPONSIBLE

If the claim brought against you was in fact caused by a third party, you should contact the clerk of the court for an explanation of how you may bring a crossaction or third-party action. Here's an example of such a case: An action was brought against a contractor who made repairs on a home. The homeowner claimed that the bathroom repairs were improper, as some tiles were coming loose. The general contractor who was hired to do the remodeling had subcontracted the tiling repair to a bathroom-tile specialist. The homeowner, merely wanting to be reimbursed for the faulty repair, brought claim against the general contractor whom he had hired. After receiving notice of the claim, the general contractor brought a third-party action against the bathroom-tile specialist. All three went to court.

Even though the claim may be found to be valid against the general contractor, the general contractor will be reimbursed by the bathroom tile company for any award because the tile company was put on notice by the person originally sued, the general contractor.

There are also cases in which, by contract, you are indemnified for any loss. This means another person has agreed to pay any such claims that are the result of something you have done. One such type of contract is the one you probably hold with the company that insures your car. For an annual fee (insurance premium), your insurance company has agreed to indemnify you for whatever liabilities you incur as the result of the operation of your automobile, van, or truck (see Chapter XI, "Negligence"). If you are sued following an automobile accident, it is important to notify your insurance carrier, who will probably want to appear with you in court. If you do not notify your insurance carrier and appear on your own behalf, the insurance company may not reimburse you for any award made against you.

CHECKLIST IF A CLAIM HAS BEEN BROUGHT AGAINST YOU

- Accept your mail. (If you refuse mail from Small Claims Court, a default judgment may be awarded against you.)
- Find out who is suing you. Write down the court date, place, and time.
- Contact the person who is suing you.
- If the claim is valid, attempt to settle it, and remember to inform the court clerk of any settlement.
- Prepare your case.
- It is very important to appear on time on your court date (even early).
- Answer "Ready" when called.
- Before the case begins, present any counterclaim you may have against the person who made the claim.
- Pay attention to the facts presented.
- Present your facts and any documents in logical order.
- Respond directly if the judge asks you questions.
- Do not use any legal language you may know.
- Ask questions of your opponent.
- Ask questions of opposing witnesses.

CHAPTER

V
———◆———

After You Have Completed the Presentation

THE DECISION

THE JUDGE HAS asked if there is anything further either party would like to say. By this time you have completed your presentation and hope the judge understands all the facts necessary to decide the case in your favor. Both you and your opponent have answered the judge's questions. If you are still talking and the judge indicates that enough has been said, take his word for it and wrap up your presentation quickly. At the conclusion of testimony, the judge has reviewed all of the physical evidence and any documents you have presented and may now be in a position to render a decision or award.

Small Claims Court litigants deserve and get decisions within a short period of time. The decision will either award a sum of money or not.

If the court finds in favor of the claimant against the respondent for damages, then the person filing the claim has been successful in his or her case. The decision is stated in an explicit sum of money. The court may also award interest dating from the time the event occurred until the present. This would depend on the amount of money owed and the length of time that has passed.

After You Have Completed the Presentation

When the claimant wins, any court costs incurred will also be added to the award. This is usually the small filing fee and any extra monies charged for service of notices or subpoenas.

If no award is made in favor of the person who brought the claim, it is because the court finds in favor of the respondent against the claimant: *no cause for action*. This simply means that there is no basis for the claim and no money award is being granted.

Sometime the judge reserves decision. This means the decision will be made shortly after the court appearance and mailed to the parties. In a rare case, the judge will write a lengthy decision explaining his or her reasons for the decision. This is done because the judge would like to emphasize a certain point to either party or because the judge believes they deserve a full explanation of the verdict.

The decision will be stated in simple language saying that the judge finds in favor of one party or the other and indicating the sum, if there is a money award given. Judges who render decisions from the bench (at the time the case is heard) often give a short explanation of the reason behind a decision. If the person who brought the claim is successful, the judge may ask the losing party when he will pay the amount awarded or what arrangements can be worked out regarding a payment schedule.

Do not be surprised if the judge tells you that the decision will not be made from the bench but will be *reserved*. High emotion in the courtroom often causes a judge to reserve decision. When the presentations are emotional, people's states of mind may make it impossible for them to accept a rational decision. (There have been times when actual fights have broken out in Small Claims Court.) A thoughtful judge will reserve decision when it appears that the hostility in the courtroom may result in a further emotional outcry from either party.

Another reason the judge may reserve decision is to give additional consideration to all of the facts. He or she will review all of the documents, evidence, and the judge's notes. Certain questions may require legal research.

If decision is reserved in your case, be patient. You will receive the decision soon and will know that your case has received very careful attention.

Small Claims Court must award sums of money. On occasion, as earlier indicated, a judge may order a certain act to be performed. Failure to do the act will result in an award of money damages. An example is the case of two roommates. Beth and Jill were living together and had an argument. Jill moved out and took a wall hanging that belonged to Beth. Beth sued for the value of the wall hanging, $350. After both parties testified, the judge believed that the item belonged to Beth and asked Jill if she would be willing to return it. She said yes, if the judge so ordered. The judge gave her fifteen days to return the item. If she failed to return the item, he indicated that an award would be made for $350 together with court costs. This alternative type of decision is very effective. If the item were not returned, Beth would simply call the court clerk and the award of $350 would be made. Jill would then be notified of this judgment by mail.

COLLECTING THE AWARD

Congratulations! You have won in Small Claims Court! What do you do now to collect your award?

At the same time you learned of the decision, your opponent was also notified. You should contact your opponent by mail and advise him or her of the decision as well, asking for payment within ten days. The respondent will usually pay the sum either to you directly or to the court. In some courts the clerk will accept a check from the losing party and place it in the court account. Once the monies have cleared the bank, the clerk will issue a check to you.

Studies have shown that most judgments in Small Claims

After You Have Completed the Presentation

Court are paid voluntarily. Default judgments usually cause the most problems. In these cases, the respondent not only failed to appear in court, but also does not wish to comply with the court's decision.

If your opponent does not pay voluntarily the amount awarded, there are certain steps you should take to collect the money. Seek out the court enforcement officer—a marshal, sheriff, constable, or court officer. They are all civil enforcement officers who deal with civil awards and orders of the court. The officer will not take action unless you make the request. He or she will want to know what assets the respondent has, where the respondent works, what bank accounts exist in the name of the respondent, and the location of any personal property that may be available to satisfy the judgment.

The court officer will obtain a document called an execution of judgment from the clerk and notify the respondent that he or she should pay the sum. If the payment is still not made, the court officer may seize any assets, tie up any bank accounts, file an execution against personal property, or levy upon the wages of the respondent in the amount of 10 percent of the gross wages earned. If the respondent is self-employed, the court may order an installment payment order for a certain amount to be paid each week to the court officer. Additionally, if the respondent has real property such as land, a home, or a building, you should file the judgment in the county clerk's office or with the property registrar in the locale of the property. The judgment would then act as a lien against the real property, which then could not be transferred until the judgment is paid in full. If a judgment is not paid promptly, interest from the date of the award to time of payment may be added.

Once you have been paid either voluntarily or with the help of the court enforcement officer, you are required by law to advise the clerk of the Small Claims Court in writing. You should also inform any other place where you have filed a judgment that the amount has been paid in full. This is called filing a satisfaction. Your failure to do so may result in a violation of the criminal law in your state, since it may unjustifiably affect the credit record of the person against whom an award was made.

IF YOU LOSE

If a decision is rendered against you requiring you to pay a sum of money to the claimant, you should pay promptly. If you are unable to pay in a lump sum, you should contact the court clerk or your opponent and work out a payment schedule. Your alternative to payment is an appeal, which is, at best, a long shot.

APPEALS ARE DISCOURAGED

If you are dissatisfied because your claim was dismissed or the amount awarded was not enough, you may appeal. It is rare, however, that a judgment in Small Claims Court is modified or reversed by a higher court. Appeals are often heard without either party being present. The new decision is based upon the record that was made at the time you appeared in Small Claims Court. No new evidence is permitted at the appeal level; no new testimony is taken. Your *only day in court* is at the time of the original hearing. Higher-court judges review the transcript of the proceedings to determine whether substantial justice has been done. If general rules of evidence had not been followed, but the decision was just and fair, there will be no revision of the decision.

If you do choose to appeal, you must check immediately with the Small Claims Court to determine the time limit for filing the necessary notice of appeal. This is usually twenty or thirty days. You will be asked to post a bond, paying the court clerk

After You Have Completed the Presentation

the amount of money of the award to be held pending the appeal. This guarantees payment to the winning party in the event the appeal does not change the original award. Even though an appeal is permitted, it is very important that you prepare your case well for the one time it is heard by the Small Claims Court judge. You won't be heard again.

PART TWO

The Cases

Now that you are familiar with the process in Small Claims Court, you are ready to step into the courtroom with the author. With him you can hear the wide variety of cases that come to Small Claims Court, the cases that will help you prepare for your own day in court.

The types of claims you will learn about in this section include breach of contract, including separation agreements; failure to pay for services; your insurance company's failure to pay you as the insured; landlord-tenant cases, including return of security deposit; defective merchandise and resulting damages; defective installation; improper services and repairs performed, as well as those that were unnecessarily performed; negligence by automobile driver or tradesman; the heartbreak cases resulting from broken relationships; actions by infants (people under legal age); lawsuits against municipalities for unfulfilled contracts or negligence; and the area of intentional damage and missing goods.

Although you may not find a specific case that addresses the area in which you are currently interested, you can look for the case that is closest to yours and you will get a sense of how to proceed. You can imitate the most successful claimants and avoid the pitfalls of the others. It is suggested that you read all of the cases, as they will be generally helpful to you, even if they're not your area of concern today. They may be tomorrow!

Checklists in each case area will help you in preparing and presenting your claim. Use these checklists as guides, as starting points; then consider the judge's rationale in each case. It will help you to anticipate questions you may face in your own court appearance.

Although the case areas are clearly divided, there is some overlapping. For example, there is a section on negligence and one on actions by infants; both areas consider negligence, but are set off so that you can see some of the kinds of cases that children bring to Small Claims Court. The section on heartbreak cases also contains cases that could be included in other areas, but because of the relationship of the parties, they are readily classified as involving "heartbreak."

All of the cases listed are actual cases that have been heard by the author (names of the parties have been changed). Although they cite only one judge's opinion, there is a consistency that is representative of the thinking in all Small Claims Court cases.

As you learn from the experience of others, you will be much better prepared when your own case is called.

CHAPTER

VI

Contracts; Breach of Obligations to Perform

IF YOU HAVE EVER signed your name on the dotted line, chances are you are obligating yourself to perform under a contract. You may be required to pay some person a sum of money in exchange for services. You may have entered a contract to purchase goods. Some written contracts resolve disputes between people and settle their differences in a financial way; for example, setting out a couple's future obligations in a separation agreement. If either side does not live up to the terms of a contract or agreement, it is deemed breached or broken. The other party may then bring an action to enforce the contract. If the result sought is a sum of money, Small Claims Court is the proper court.

Cases in this chapter deal with the enforcement of broken separation agreements; failure to perform services as agreed when a deposit was given; and the enforcement of promissory notes.

Contracts do not have to be in writing. If you paid money based upon a representation, and the other party did not follow through on their representation, you would have a Small Claims

Court action to get your money back (as pointed out later in this chapter).

Other types of contracts to be found later in this book include your insurance company's failure to pay you as the insured; and the contractual relationship between landlords and tenants.

SEPARATION AGREEMENTS

A separation agreement is a contract between a husband and wife who no longer wish to live together. It establishes the property rights and financial obligations of each party. Often such an agreement will stipulate a certain amount of alimony or child support to be paid periodically by the husband to the wife. In some states, either spouse may be responsible for payment of certain monies to the other. Even though a subsequent divorce decree may have been granted in favor of either or both of the parties, the separation agreement continues to be a valid and binding contract between them.

If the man or woman has failed to live up to the payment schedule according to the agreement, the other may, within the monetary jurisdiction of Small Claims Court, bring an action. The husband, for example, may wish to harass his wife by delaying payments. He may believe that his wife will not do anything about this tardiness because of the expense of hiring an attorney to help her collect. Once a spouse learns that Small Claims Court is inexpensive and available, the incidence of late payments will diminish greatly.

The key to bringing an action in Small Claims Court on a separation agreement is not to let the overdue amount exceed the limits of jurisdiction. If a spouse is late by only a few weeks, there is no reason why a Small Claims Court action cannot be brought to enforce the contract and require payment of the amount due. This would nip the problem in the bud, before the small problem became a hardship to either the man or the

Contracts; Breach of Obligations to Perform

woman (or their children). If this action were brought in regular court and negotiated through attorneys, the matter would change considerably. By the time the court ordered payments brought up to date again, more time would have passed, legal fees would have mounted, and bad feelings would have gotten worse. Lawyers believe that Small Claims Court is a good alternative for keeping each party in compliance with the separation agreement.

If the amount claimed is actually owed, the spouse owing the amount should pay the debt and meet future obligations promptly. It is best to settle out of court if possible. If the matter must go to court, the parties should be careful what they state before the judge. The judge is interested in only one issue: whether the money specified in the Agreement is owed or not. Extraneous matters between the parties regarding the nature of their unfortunate, broken relationship are irrelevant.

In preparation for court, you should copy the appropriate section of the separation agreement, highlighting the clause specifying payments. The original agreement should be brought to court as well, so that the judge can examine the signatures. A list of the payments made and their dates, together with an indication of the missed payments, should be typed or printed clearly. If you are sued, you should bring your ledger, which lists in a chronological order the amounts paid, the specific dates of those payments, and the dates on which future payments will become due. Also bring copies of your canceled checks.

Sally Sherman v. *Marvin Sherman*
CLAIM: Alimony arrears

The parties entered the courtroom, each armed with a briefcase. There were no other witnesses. Sally Sherman stepped up to the bar in front of the judge and stated that she was bringing this action against her ex-husband for his failure to pay certain amounts of alimony and child support. She said that Marvin was to pay the sum of $100 per week alimony, plus $100 per week child support, for a total of $200 per week. She indicated that he had made his payments on time for two years, but five weeks ago he stopped paying the alimony and only paid the child support. She presented the separation agreement, with the clause requiring both alimony and child support highlighted. She also provided a typed statement of all of the payments made since the couple had separated. The statement showed that during the last five weeks only $100 per week was paid; the checks indicated child support, not alimony.

When it was his turn, Marvin explained to the judge that this, in fact, was true. He said he did not pay the alimony for the past five weeks because he learned that Sally was going South on a midwinter vacation. He stated that if *she* could go on a vacation, she obviously did not need to have continued alimony payments. Immediately, Sally became infuriated and started to list the vacations that Marvin had taken within the past two years with his girlfriend, including trips to Europe, Hawaii, and Mexico. Each lashed out at the other.

The judge could see immediately that the couple's ill feelings had not eased since their separation. The judge told them that the divorce had already been heard and decided in another court and that the only matter appropriate to Small Claims Court was whether or not the contract they had agreed to was being obeyed. A Small Claims Court judge does not hear divorces or modifications of separation agreements; but he or she can interpret a contract and award damages to whomever is not living up to the contract.

In this case, Marvin had admitted that he had not obeyed. The judge indicated that Marvin agreed to a contract in divorce court and now must abide by it, regardless of his feelings. He was advised that if he wanted to try to amend his agreement, he could go to an appropriate court and argue his case there. But as far as the Small Claims Court judge was concerned, the agreement was valid and Marvin was required to pay back alimony in the total sum of $500.

More than just a financial matter may have been settled by the Shermans coming to Small Claims Court. Sally had proven to Marvin that she won't let him get away with his own interpretation of an agreement that both parties had negotiated. Marvin had expressed his displeasure at Sally's enjoying a vacation.

Although Marvin was clearly wrong in not making the payments under the contract, it is perhaps better that this couple brought this matter to Small Claims Court for airing rather than allowing an ongoing hatred of which the only victim could be their child.

Result: In the case of *Sally Sherman* v. *Marvin Sherman,* judgment in favor of the claimant against the respondent in the full amount of $500, plus the costs of the court.

After the award of the money damages, the judge did take a few moments to discuss with each party the importance of putting the past behind them, living according to their agreement, and carrying on their own separate and full lives.

A party to a separation agreement can bring other actions to enforce the terms of the contract. When Ann and Bill Sutton separated, they wished to provide two weeks of summer camp for each of their daughters. They had agreed to split the cost. During the past summer, Bill, as he customarily did, paid the full amount of the bill of $500. When he asked his former wife, Ann, for reimbursement of one half, she refused, stating that he had more money than she did and that she didn't wish to pay any more. Bill brought his claim to Small Claims Court and was successful. Even though in Ann's opinion Bill was better able to bear the burden of camp tuition, she had made an agreement and she was bound by its terms.

Separation agreements survive a divorce decree. This means that even though the parties were divorced, the enforcement of the terms of the separation agreement dealing with a sum of money may be heard in Small Claims Court.

If, on the other hand, there never was a separation agreement, and the terms of a divorce decree were resolved at a trial, the terms of the divorce decree may be enforced only by the court that awarded the decree. Small Claims Court can enforce the terms of an agreement or contract, but not an order of a higher court. Only the court that granted that decree can enforce its terms.

CHECKLIST FOR CLAIMANT

- Separation agreement with clause requiring payments and the amount highlighted.
- Ledger of payments made and their dates.

CHECKLIST FOR RESPONDENT

- Ledger of the amounts paid.
- Copy of canceled checks in order, proving payments were made on specific dates.

PROMISSORY NOTES

Another form of agreement between parties is a promissory note. One person gives another a sum of money and in exchange obtains a written promise to repay within a specific period of time or on demand. Herman Toole loaned Jack Leach $1,000. Jack promised to repay the money within ninety days. Herman had him sign a promissory note indicating that the $1,000 would be due in ninety days with no interest. Jack Leach kept asking for more time, and finally Herman said no, as he noted that Jack had just purchased a brand-new stereo system. Herman Toole then proceeded to Small Claims Court and simply presented the promissory note in court. Jack Leach

Contracts; Breach of Obligations to Perform 57

had no defense. He said that Herman told him he could pay it back any time he wanted to, but in this case, the note spoke for itself. Any oral agreement between the parties cannot change the fixed terms written in a promissory note.

Often, people come into Small Claims Court without evidence of a debt in the form of a promissory note. In that case, the check that was given from one party to the other should be evidence of the debt. If cash was given instead, witnesses would certainly be required to aid in the proof of the debt.

Sometimes, one person will give money to another without any intention of getting it back. This often happens in a case in which the people have a close relationship. When the relationship dissolves, the gift suddenly becomes a loan (as in the "heartbreak" case of *Millie Hagger* v. *William Short,* in Chapter XII).

CHECKLIST FOR MONEY LOANED—CLAIMANT

- Promissory note.
- If no promissory note, canceled check or cash receipt.
- If no canceled check or cash receipt, witnesses to the loan of the money.
- Any letters or written documents from the respondent that acknowledge the debt.

CHECKLIST FOR MONEY OWED—RESPONDENT

- Any papers or documents to show that the claimant never expected repayment.
- Witnesses to substantiate your defense.

FAILURE TO FULFILL CONTRACT

Unlike a promise to pay back borrowed money, as in a promissory note, or an agreement to perform services in exchange for money, an implied or unwritten promise can be made orally. One party agrees to do something and the other party anticipates it. When the promise is not fulfilled, the resulting disappointment and anger echo through the courtroom, as in the case of Margaret Lavender.

Margaret Lavender v. *Trailhound Escorted Tours, Inc.*
CLAIM: Misrepresented tour service

Margaret Lavender was a widow in her early seventies who loved to travel. Although volunteer work kept her busy, she looked forward several times each year to vacations in other parts of the country. She enjoyed learning about the history of the different areas, visiting landmarks, meeting new people, and enjoying new friendships. She found the best way for her to travel was on an escorted bus tour.

It was in the fall of the year when Margaret saw an advertisement for Trailhound Escorted Tours, Inc. Although she had never gone with Trailhound before, she went to their business office and met with Bob Wetmore, the tour agent. She told him that she wanted to take a nine-day tour through the mountains of New England during the autumn changing of the foliage. Mr. Wetmore told her that that tour had been filled, but she could take the eleven-day tour to Nova Scotia. Margaret liked that idea, as long as the tour was escorted. She felt that the $890 for the tour should include a driver *and* an escort to inform the tourists about the areas they would be passing through and generally entertain them. Her hopes were that within a few days all the people on the bus would become friends. Bob assured her that the escort, Alma Goodsite, was experienced and would do an excellent job.

Mrs. Lavender was very enthusiastic and said to Mr. Wetmore, "Although I would rather be going on the New England tour, I will take this other tour as long as the driver does the

Contracts; Breach of Obligations to Perform 59

driving, the escort does the talking, and there is music on the bus." She was assured that this would be the case.

Margaret arrived at the bus station, said good-bye to her family, and got on the bus anticipating a lovely vacation. As soon as the bus pulled out, the driver introduced himself as Buzz Guyer and then introduced the hostess, whose name was Helen Huntley. Immediately, Mrs. Lavender was curious as to why Alma Goodsite, whom she had heard so much about, had not come. She never found out. What she did find out, after the first two days, was that Miss Huntley was merely a vacationing office worker. Her only responsibility on the tour was to pass out candy and make certain the passengers stayed together. When questioned about the history of the area they passed through, she said she was unfamiliar with it, but would attempt to make the tourists as comfortable as possible.

Immediately, Mrs. Lavender decided this tour was not for her! For hours on end, the bus rolled along without a word from either the driver or the hostess, and the only music Margaret heard was church music played on Sunday morning.

Once on the third day when the bus stopped, Margaret attempted to call the main office of Trailhound Escorted Tours, Inc., and got no answer. She tried again on the fourth day with the same result. On the fifth day, she called Bob Wetmore, the tour agent, at his home, and told him she was very disappointed with the tour. It was not an escorted tour as promised and she wanted to come home.

Mr. Wetmore told her, "No, you stay with the tour because you are our responsibility. When you come home, we'll discuss a refund." Mrs. Lavender said that she would accept that, but that she was most disappointed.

Upon returning home after the completion of the tour, she went to Bob Wetmore's office to discuss a refund. He told her he had talked it over with the owners of Trailhound and was told it was not company policy to issue refunds. He was sorry she did not enjoy the tour but "we can't please everybody."

Margaret Lavender then filed a claim in Small Claims Court for a full refund. She related her story and brought the brochure showing that the tours were escorted and guaranteed to be most enjoyable. She brought along Alice, a friend she had made on the tour. Alice said that she had made many tours with this company, but this one was different. Obviously something had gone wrong with this tour.

Bob Wetmore, who no longer worked for Trailhound Escorted Tours, Inc., was subpoenaed by Mrs. Lavender. He admitted that he did promise an escorted tour with educational conversation by Alma Goodsite. At the last moment, however, she had a change in plans and had to go on another tour, so the hostess was added as a fill-in. He said that the company was unable to give the refund because it bore the expenses of lodging, food, and transportation as well as tour fees. He said it was unfortunate that Mrs. Lavender did not enjoy the trip, but since many others had, it was just a matter of opinion.

The Judge then asked Margaret if she enjoyed any part of the trip. She said that some of the side tours were interesting, but that if she had known that the escort would not be along, she would never have paid the large sum of money for an eleven-day trip.

Result: In the case of *Margaret Lavender* v. *Trailhound Escorted Tours, Inc.,* an award was granted in favor of the claimant against the respondent in the amount of $400.

The judge felt that the tour was not accurately represented by the respondent. Mrs. Lavender had specifically stated that she would go on the tour only if a good escort would be traveling with the group. When the company changed the plans to include a hostess with no experience, Mrs. Lavender's condition of accepting the tour was not fulfilled. The judge did not award the full amount of the claim because Margaret received some benefit from the tour. He also considered the fact that she did not make her objection known to the company until nearly halfway through the tour.

If Margaret had not made the specific request for an escorted tour, then she would have had no cause for action. Here the tour representative was fully aware of her specific request.

CHECKLIST FOR CLAIMANT

- Brochure or advertisement.
- Receipt or canceled check.
- Any witnesses who were with claimant.
- Witnesses who made the representations and upon whom you relied.

SERVICES CONTRACTED FOR BUT NOT PERFORMED

Has anybody told you that he or she would do something for a certain price and asked you for a portion of it in advance? Sometimes this happens when you take your shoes for repair. If the repairman doesn't know you, he might want half the bill paid in advance. If you came back several weeks later and the work wasn't done, not only would you ask for your shoes back, but your deposit as well.

Storeowners who have been in business for a while often continue to create good will by doing their work properly. On the other hand, door-to-door salesmen who ask you to sign a contract may never be seen again. Unlike your friendly neighborhood merchant, you can't "go back" with something that isn't right. While they may have had very good intentions at the time they entered the contract (and took half of your money for a deposit), they often disappear. You are left with no merchandise and a lighter wallet. This almost happened to Steve and Debbie Philips.

Stephen Philips v. Jerry West
CLAIM: Return of deposit from painter

Steve Philips bought a once-elegant older home in need of extensive renovation. He spent several months tearing out rotted wood, old wiring, and plumbing. He rewired the grand home, completely remodeled the kitchen, installed new bathrooms, and restored the interior wood trim to its original beauty. He had worked day and night turning the place into a comfortable home of which he and his new wife, Debbie, could be proud.

After completing the interior, he told Debbie that next year's project would be to paint the home's exterior, which was sorely in need of scraping, burning, sanding, priming, and painting. Debbie insisted that he had done enough work; it was now time to relax and let someone else complete the job. She saw an ad in the paper for a painter who claimed to be experienced. Jerry West, a dapper, middle-aged man, responded to Debbie's call. After considerable preliminary conversation, Jerry looked over the house with Steve and Debbie and told them he could do the job for $1,200, if they bought the paint. A contract was drawn up at the agreed price indicating that it would be completed within "a reasonable time." This was in June. Jerry also required one half of the price in advance, so Steve gave him a check for that amount. About a week later, Jerry arrived with two helpers who unloaded three ladders, several old paint cans, and a few brushes, which he put in the Philips' garage.

Several more days passed, but Jerry was nowhere to be seen. The Philips called him several times, but there was no answer. Finally, in mid-August Steve Philips talked with Mr. West's wife, Penny. She said that her husband was having truck trouble and was stranded on another job. She promised he would be at the house soon. By Labor Day, the only progress that had been made was one afternoon's scraping and sanding on the first floor.

By the end of September, the Philipses decided that Mr. West

Contracts; Breach of Obligations to Perform

had not lived up to his end of the contract. They advised him in writing that the contract was canceled and he should return the deposit and take his materials from the garage. He called them and said he was very busy on other jobs, but that he did spend a great deal of time on their job and would finish it sometime in the next week.

He didn't appear at all.

The Philipses then brought this claim to Small Claims Court to recover the amount of the deposit. In the meantime, they got an estimate for $1,350 from another painter who was willing to start immediately.

In court, Philips presented the contract, the canceled check for the deposit, and photographs of the house showing its poor exterior condition. He demanded a full refund.

Jerry West said that he and his helpers had been on the job and spent at least a whole day that was worth at least $200. He also told the judge he wanted a chance to finish the job.

Steve Philips said that he had already hired another painter and presented the estimate. Also in the estimate was a statement showing that the amount of work that had been done by Mr. West was worth only about $25. West then said that the contract allowed him "a reasonable time" to complete the job and he had every intention of completing it within a reasonable time. As proof of that, he added, he even left his ladders in the garage of the Philips' house.

Result: In the case of *Stephen Philips* v. *Jerry West,* judgment was granted for Stephen Philips in the amount of $575 plus interest from the time of the payment of the deposit.

In this case, the contract should have been more specific regarding exactly how many days Mr. West would have to complete the job. The judge had to interpret what was meant by "a reasonable time." He reasoned this way: The house-painting season does not last much beyond October and it appeared that, even though the ladders were left in the garage, the painter had no intention of doing the work during that painting season.

This case is an example of certain unreliable contractors, home-improvement companies, and tradespeople who collect half of a value of a job and then either never deliver the product or service, or delay it far beyond a reasonable length of time. This is the type of case in which you must act quickly if you have a claim. If you wait too long, they may in fact go out of business and take off with your money.

Checklist for Claimant

- Original contract.
- Photographs of house or work to be done showing what was left undone.
- Estimate of another tradesperson to do the work, including estimate of what had been done by previous worker.
- Witnesses to any conversation.

Checklist for Respondent

- Original contract.
- Any modification of original contract to show extension of time.
- Documentation of extenuating circumstances preventing you from proceeding.
- Witnesses to any conversation.

CHAPTER

VII

Your Insurance Company's Failure to Pay You as the Insured

EACH TIME YOU purchase insurance to protect yourself against a casualty or loss, you are entering into a contract with the insurance company. In exchange for your paying an annual premium, the insurance company agrees to reimburse you for any loss you suffer as a result of certain actions. In addition to medical insurance, there is insurance for life, accident, damage to your automobile, general liability, and homeowner's or renter's insurance. You can contract with the insurance company to purchase any type of protection you desire.

If you have suffered a loss that is covered according to your policy, you make a claim and should recover the amount of your loss.

There are times that you and the insurance company adjuster are unable to agree on the proper amount for which you should be reimbursed. You believe that a wall hanging that was stolen or destroyed in a fire may be worth $5,000, although the company may determine that it was worth only $2,500. If the amount involved is large, you should hire an attorney and bring an action in a regular term of court against your own insurance company.

But most insurance claims are for small amounts. Although most companies are fair in dealing with their insured, there are, sometimes, disagreements. Such was the case of Dick and Sylvia Flood.

CLAIMS AGAINST HOMEOWNER'S OR RENTER'S INSURANCE COMPANY

Dick and Sylvia Flood v. *AA Insurance Company*
CLAIM: Failure to pay claim for flood damage in home

The Flood family rarely went on vacation and had looked forward to a two-week trip to the seashore. After a great deal of elaborate preparation, Mr. and Mrs. Flood and their two children packed the family station wagon, secured their house by double-bolting all the doors, and headed off to the coast. Because of an elaborate new lock system that they installed in their home several weeks earlier, they didn't ask any members of the family to check their house while they were away. They believed that all would be secure.

After a wonderful vacation, they arrived back home. As their young son John unlocked the back door of the house near the laundry-room area, a flood of water came rushing down the garage steps. He yelled for his mom and dad; Dick and Sylvia came running. As they entered the house, they found that a pipe had burst in the laundry room adjacent to the kitchen. Water was pouring out and several inches covered the entire floor of their large home. Dick rushed to the basement only to find himself knee-deep in water. They immediately turned off the water main; then they called the local fire department to pump out the basement; and finally they mopped the floors dry. Soon after, they called a plumber, who repaired a $12 rubber hose.

Days later, they assessed the damage and found that aside from the aggravation and hours of cleanup, the only real damage

Your Insurance Company's Failure to Pay You

was a buckled kitchen floor. The flooring material was a high-priced vinyl, which they had put down only a year before at a cost of $650. They obtained estimates to take up the damaged floor and replace it with the same material. They were shocked to learn that in one year's time the price had increased to $900.

Relying on their insurance to help them, they called their agent, who sent the adjuster from AA Insurance Company. Leon Chysl arrived within an hour, inspected the property, and asked the Floods if any property had been damaged in the basement. They said that the only damage that appeared serious was the kitchen floor. Mr. Chysl said that they would certainly be covered under their homeowner's insurance.

The Floods then presented him with the estimates of repair. Chysl stated he would pay only the amount that the floor originally cost, not the amount to replace it, even though their homeowner's policy specified reimbursement of replacement cost. The Floods told Chysl that the price had escalated to the sum of $900 in a year and that the old floor had to be removed.

The insurance company adjuster responded, "Well, the old floor has some salvage value. You could probably sell the pieces at a garage sale."

The Floods were furious! Although Dick Flood felt like hitting the adjuster, Sylvia told him to relax and take the matter to Small Claims Court.

As the Flood family of four appeared in court, so did the insurance company adjuster, Leon Chysl. The Floods presented their case, telling how they had acted quickly on their arrival to lessen their damage. They said they believed that the insurance policy would cover them for exactly this type of loss. Dick Flood said they could have made any kind of claim, but were totally honest in stating that the only damage they truly suffered was the replacement of the badly buckled kitchen floor. He produced photographs of the floor showing how it had heaved and cracked. He then told the cost of original installation, as well as a verified estimate of replacement from the same company. He circled that part of the insurance policy that showed that *replacement cost* of the item should be given to the insured. Each of his children and his wife then explained what they did to clean up the house and keep the damage to a minimum. The youngsters told of taking all of their toys outside and letting them dry in the sun instead of throwing them away.

Then it was Leon Chysl's turn. He said he didn't care what the policy said, it was his company's practice to pay only the original cost of the installation. He felt he was being generous in this case because he didn't depreciate the value of the floor because of its age. Chysl went on to say that somebody would purchase the scraps of the floor, perhaps in a garage sale.

Dick Flood then jumped up and asked Chysl if he would like to buy it. He would sell it to him for anything he would pay for it.

Chysl was silent.

The judge asked to see the policy, which said that the insurance company agreed "to reimburse for any loss as the reasonable value of the item at the time of the loss."

Result: In the case of *Dick and Sylvia Flood* v. *AA Insurance Company,* judgment was granted in favor of the claimants in the full amount of $900, including tax, together with the filing fee. Interest was also awarded because of the size of the award and time the parties spent attempting to settle the matter before court became necessary.

The Floods did everything to lessen the potential claim against the insurance company. The insurance company had an obligation, according to the terms of the policy, to reimburse the Floods for any loss based upon its reasonable value. The Court determined that reasonable value means the actual replacement cost at the time of the loss. The judge believed that requiring the Floods to salvage the broken floor was going a bit too far. The Floods prepared their case well and Chysl had no defense.

Your Insurance Company's Failure to Pay You

Other cases have come to Small Claims Court regarding interpretation of the homeowner's or renter's insurance policy. They have included disputes over repair of fire damage in a kitchen; theft of certain items from a house; and storm damage, such as ice causing gutters to fall, or trees hitting houses and causing damage. Each of these cases requires you to contact your insurance company to determine the reimbursement for your loss under the terms of the policy.

Read your policy carefully to determine exactly what is covered. Most will consider the age of the item to be replaced. For example, if an appliance is damaged as the result of a fire, you may be covered by your policy. If the appliance would cost $500 to replace but was fifteen years old, your insurance company may properly consider the age and the future use that can be expected from such an appliance. The depreciation factor could be taken into account on any item. The appliance may have a life of only fifteen years, and if you have used it all of that time and then seek to replace it with a brand-new one, this would be unreasonable and unfair. Bringing a claim to Small Claims Court in such a matter would result in a judgment of "no cause for action," if the insurance company raised the defense of depreciation.

On the other hand, if you can prove that the appliance was never used and was still in its original carton, you may be entitled to all of the value of the appliance. Each case is determined on its own merits. It is important, however, that you document your case carefully so that you can prove each and every element.

CHECKLIST FOR CLAIMANT

- Original invoice or receipt for item claimed damaged.
- Photographs of damaged goods before damage, if possible.
- Photographs of damage (if possible bring item to court).
- Invoice showing replacement cost including labor and *tax*.

- Present any witnesses who observed item or helped you lessen damage.

CLAIMS AGAINST YOUR HEALTH INSURANCE

How many times have you made a claim on your health insurance and had a response from an impersonal computer?

Health care has become so expensive that everyone needs to have some kind of medical insurance. Group insurance plans enable each of the subscribers to share the burdensome cost of unforeseen illness.

There are two types of plans. The most common is the general community type of insurance to which a person may subscribe individually or in a group through an employer. In many cases, a fringe benefit of employment is health insurance.

A second type of plan, which is becoming more popular, is complete medical and dental insurance coverage. This covers all medical and dental treatment, including that for an emergency injury, catastrophic illness, or routine medical and dental care. In this plan, there is no deductible, and the subscriber pays only an annual fee. Medical care is often delivered through a clinic or health center at which the subscriber may not have an individual doctor, but will be seen by a team of physicians on a rotating basis.

In both plans, it is stipulated that certain health-care functions will be performed for a single annual fee. In the first type of plan described, the subscriber is reimbursed for medical expenses according to a scheduled amount. In the second type of plan, the subscriber is provided service directly by the medical staff affiliated with the plan. In certain cases, there may be reimbursement for a subscriber who is attended by doctors or dentists who are not affiliated with the plan's medical center. In many cases, however, subscribers will not be covered for such "outside" care. It is in this area that disputes can arise, as in the case of Richard Fertig.

Richard Fertig v. Complete Health Care, Inc.
CLAIM: Reimbursement for medical expenses

Richard Fertig's employer provided medical coverage by Complete Health Care, Inc., as a fringe benefit of employment. Any time Mr. Fertig needed medical or dental treatment he would go to a clinic operated by the Complete Health Care, Inc., plan. This worked out well for several months.

At about nine-thirty one July evening, Mr. Fertig was attending a baseball game with two of his friends when he suddenly got a pain in his side. The pain got progressively worse until he was unable to stand up straight. His two friends, with the assistance of a police officer, immediately took him to the nearest hospital.

When he entered the emergency department, he described his symptoms to the admitting nurse, gave his name and address, and was immediately taken in for treatment. He couldn't stand up and was too ill to sign any documents. He was in such pain that he was seen ahead of many people who had been waiting for treatment. After examining Mr. Fertig, doctors determined that he was passing a kidney stone through his system. They gave him medication for his pain. During the one hour in the hospital, Mr. Fertig did pass the stone and the pain subsided. He was released from the emergency department shortly thereafter, and completed all of the usual paperwork on his way out. On the documents, he indicated his association with Complete Health Care, Inc. The hospital submitted the bill for $387.52 to the plan.

Mr. Fertig was notified by the hospital and the plan that payment was rejected. The form letter stated that Complete Health Care, Inc., would take care of illnesses only if treated by an approved plan physician or illnesses creating a life-threatening emergency. The information that had been given to Complete Health Care, Inc., indicated that Mr. Fertig did not seek an approved plan physician (none of whom were available at the hospital's emergency department) and that a kidney stone was not a life-threatening emergency. The form letter went on to say that before receiving treatment he expected the plan to cover, he should have received authorization from the plan.

Mr. Fertig wrote again to the plan that he believed that his illness was a "life-threatening emergency." His response was a computer printout indicating that his claim had been rejected. When he contacted the administration of Complete Health Care, Inc., he was given many names and a brushoff. Tired of getting the runaround, Mr. Fertig filed a claim in Small Claims Court.

He presented his claim by describing how the pain started and became worse. He said it became so bad at times that he didn't remember exactly what happened. He presented the unpaid hospital bill together with a copy of his hospital records. Mr. Fertig then called as witnesses the two friends who were with him at the baseball game. They told the court what they observed of his condition. Larry Hill, an administrator from the health plan, also appeared in court. Hill stated that the contract was very clear: If a condition is not a life-threatening emergency or treatment is unauthorized, the plan will not reimburse the subscriber.

Mr. Fertig turned to Mr. Hill and asked him if he had ever had a kidney stone.

Mr. Hill said that he hadn't.

Mr. Fertig described in graphic detail the pain he had suffered.

Mr. Hill winced, then sat down.

Result: In the case of *Richard Fertig* v. *Complete Health Care, Inc.,* the court decided in favor of the claimant in the full amount of $387.52. Mr. Fertig had prepared his case well by first going through the necessary channels with the insurance

Your Insurance Company's Failure to Pay You

company and learning the reason for the rejection of the claim. He then challenged their reason with a copy of the hospital records and the testimony of his friends.

One can easily be frustrated in dealing with an impersonal corporate respondent. Computers are machines which don't suffer pain, and Fertig was smart in looking for more human answers in Small Claims Court.

Many people have a general-coverage plan rather than a plan that requires you to seek certain physicians and treatment centers. Sometimes your claim can become lost and the doctor you have selected is not paid. Your doctor will seek reimbursement from you. You should pay your doctor and then seek reimbursement from the health insurance.

Ian Tenderfoot broke his ankle on the job. Several days after he received emergency medical treatment at the hospital, he developed a secondary infection. He had to go to the doctor several times, incurring additional bills totaling $325 for antibiotics, X rays, and examinations. When he submitted the bill to Blue Feather Health Services, the general plan that covered such illnesses, he was told by computer that his claim was rejected as his illness did not require emergency medical treatment. It was his contention that the infection was a result of emergency medical treatment and not an ordinary illness.

He attempted to deal with Blue Feather Health Services for several months, got nowhere, and brought his claim to Small Claims Court. His position was documented in a doctor's letter saying that the treatment resulted from the accident he had on the job. Once Blue Feather Health Services received the notice of claim from Small Claims Court, personal attention from a Blue Feather employee replaced the computer's cold response. The claim was personally reviewed and was paid before the matter was heard in court. This is an example of a matter in which the filing itself was sufficient to flush out a fair response to the claim.

Checklist for Claimant

- Copy of the policy.
- Copy of bill or claim in question.
- Rejection notice, if you receive one from your company.
- Hospital records or other documentation to dispute rejection.
- Witnesses to substantiate your claim.

CLAIMS AGAINST YOUR AUTOMOBILE INSURANCE COMPANY

When you purchase automobile insurance, it consists of two parts: liability insurance, and collision or comprehensive insurance. Liability insurance is required by law in most states. It indemnifies you for any negligence claims against you. For example, if you damage another person's property or injure them, your insurance company will indemnify you for any money you may be compelled to pay the other party.

Collision or comprehensive insurance reimburses you for any loss you suffer either as a result of your own negligence or for damage caused by an unknown person. For example, if you were in a collision and could not find another person at fault, you would be reimbursed for the damage to your vehicle by your collision or comprehensive policy. Collision or comprehensive insurance also covers you for damage to your parked car when you cannot find the culprit, and for fire or vandalism. In this type of insurance, there is usually a deductible; the insured has to pay the first $50 or $100 of the damages, but can collect the remainder. Usually your insurance company will be fair in dealing with your claim. On occasion, however, there may be a disagreement. You may wish to have new parts installed in your car to replace the old, damaged parts, but your insurance

Your Insurance Company's Failure to Pay You 75

company adjuster may disagree on the interpretation of the terms of your policy, as in David Whitaker's case.

David Whitaker v. Safety First Auto Insurance Company
CLAIM: Dispute with claimant's automobile insurance company over amount to repair

David Whitaker had recently switched his car insurance to Safety First Auto Insurance Company because of the inexpensive premium. A cautious man, he bought both the general liability policy protecting him against any loss he caused others, and the collision policy, which carried a $50 deductible clause. This clause meant that he would have to pay the first $50 of any collision damage to his own car, and Safety First would pay for the rest.

David had just purchased a new five-speed foreign car. When his brother Reggie called to say that he was in town from Philadelphia for only an hour, David hopped into his new treasure and headed for the airport to pick him up.

Unfortunately, he was in too much of a hurry. He shifted into what he thought was first gear, accelerated, and backed into a tree at the end of his driveway. The collision occurred with such force that the rear bumper of the new car was pushed in nearly a foot and a half, and the trunk lid was badly bent. David was more than annoyed. His wife, Stephanie, drove him to the airport in her car.

The next morning, David surveyed the damage. He had the car towed to the dealer from whom he had just bought it, and requested an estimate of the damage. The cost to replace the rear bumper, trunk lid, and do other repair work amounted to $719.

David then contacted Tabatha Smartly at Safety First Auto Insurance Company, who also inspected the damage to the automobile. She told David to take the car to another repair shop across town. Her company, she said, was accustomed to doing business with them. She added that they specialized in cannibalizing used parts from new automobiles that had been wrecked and speculated that they would be willing to do the work for only $450. David became extremely upset and refused to move the car. He said that he wanted to have the work done at the authorized dealer who had just sold him the car and that he was entitled to new parts.

Miss Smartly insisted that company policy dictated that he would have to go to the other shop. The terms of the insurance policy, she added, merely said "replace the parts." It did not specify new parts.

David had the work done at the authorized dealer and then brought the claim to Small Claims Court.

In court, he presented his story, noting that he had caused the damage to his car by his own negligence. Since the car was quite new, he said he wanted to replace the parts with new parts, not those that were on somebody else's automobile. He presented the insurance policy, which stated replacement would be covered, and showed his receipt for the amount paid at the garage where the work was done. He also presented the bill of sale for the automobile. David brought an action for $669, which represented the amount he paid the dealer for repairs, minus the $50 deductible. Tabatha Smartly, the claims agent for Safety First, said that a bumper from another automobile or even one that was rechromed should be satisfactory. Even if it wasn't brand new, it was just like new, she said.

Mr. Whitaker cross-examined Miss Smartly and asked her if she knew where the bumper had been, how many miles the other car had had on it, or how old the automobile was. Miss Smartly had no answer.

The judge asked to see the insurance policy, which indicated replacement was required.

Result: In the matter of *David Whitaker* v. *Safety First Auto Insurance Company,* award was granted in full for the claimant.

The insurance policy in this case did not clearly specify what "replacement" meant. The judge felt the policy could be interpreted to mean replacement with new parts or used parts. He therefore felt he should take into consideration the age of the automobile and parts that were being replaced. Since this case concerned a new car and the agent did not know how old the replacement parts would be, the judge felt that new parts should be required. If the same policy had been used in the case of an older automobile, the company might have won.

The judge further believed that David Whitaker should be able to choose the dealer who would do the work. He should not be forced to go to an inconvenient area of town and use a body shop with which he had no experience, trust, or confidence. It did not take David long to learn why Safety First Auto Insurance Company offered lower premiums. He promptly returned to his old company; the cost was higher, but the claims were fairly paid.

CHECKLIST FOR CLAIMANT

- Photographs of damage.
- Invoice showing purchase of car.
- Receipt showing payment of repair bill.
- Insurance policy highlighting clause on repair of damage under collision.

CHAPTER

VIII

Landlord-Tenant Claims

IT IS HIGHLY probable that you have been, are, or will be sometime in your life either a landlord or a tenant. The landlord is the owner of the apartment, house, or building. He or she has responsibilities of ownership, which include payment of mortgage and property maintenance, and, of course, the landlord has to come up with the capital to purchase the property in the first place. If the landlord wants to make a profit on his investment, he may rent the property. The payments that the tenant makes help the landlord meet his obligations. Any money that is left over is profit.

The property is actually like a product. The landlord has the space; the tenant desires to purchase the right to occupy it. This is done by either a written or an oral lease. A written lease spells out more definitely the obligations of both the landlord and the tenant to each other. When either party does not live up to the terms of a lease (rental agreement), it is deemed to have been breached or broken. This chapter deals with that relationship and the liability of one party to the other.

CLAIMS AGAINST LANDLORDS

At the time a tenant enters into an agreement with a landlord to rent property, the landlord will usually require a security deposit often equal to a month's rent, in addition to the first month's rent. This will be the case regardless of whether the lease is oral or in writing. The purpose of the security deposit is to protect the landlord's interest. It works in two ways: First, it will assure the landlord that there is some money being placed in escrow to require the tenant to live up to the terms of the lease; and second, it assures the landlord that after the tenant leaves, the property will be left in the same order and condition as when it was rented. The law takes into account, however, that the property may have ordinary wear and tear over time. If there are items broken or destroyed as the result of negligence of the tenant, the landlord has some money from which to deduct the amount of the damage. In other words, the security deposit serves as an inducement for the tenant to leave the property in good order.

When you move out, the landlord inspects the property to determine if there has been any damage. It is best for you, the tenant, to be present during the inspection so that there is no question about the condition of the property. Most landlords will be fair and will readily return what is due the tenant. Some, however, will deduct an excessive amount for the most minimal damage. They may even charge for nonexistent damage. Other landlords are merely very slow to return security deposits and hope that if they return only a portion of what is due or none at all, the tenant will forget about it.

Small Claims Court guards against abuse of a tenant's security deposit by giving the tenant a quick, low-cost, and efficient remedy. Often tenants move not only from residence to residence but also from one locale to another. If a landlord does not pay back the security deposit the tenant may be in another area where he or she is unable to bring a claim against the landlord. In Small Claims Court a claim can be brought in a short period of time (a matter of days) so that the failure to return the security deposit without just cause can be remedied.

If a tenant's claim is a valid one, a landlord will often pay the claim at the time the action is brought instead of coming to court. If this happens in your case, be certain that the landlord pays you the filing fee and any interest on the security deposit that your state law requires. This is usually 1 percent below the interest rate on an average day-to-day account in a savings bank. If the landlord does not settle with you prior to court, you should prepare your documentation and ask an independent witness to appear in Court with you. This should be someone who observed the condition of your property before you left it. It is important that you return your keys to the landlord or the landlord's agent when you leave the property. This represents a symbolic but significant turning over of control of the property to the landlord and prevents the landlord from claiming that he had to spend extra money to change the locks. It also shows that you have left the property at the time agreed to in your lease.

In this action, the landlord's defense would involve showing damage that occurred to the property while it was under your control. Remember, this means damage that is *above ordinary wear and tear*. Such damage might include holes in the walls where pictures were hung, excessive dirt on the carpet or flooring, a soiled bathroom, and/or broken items within the premises. If these conditions exist, the landlord is entitled to retain a certain amount of the security deposit. The landlord must prove, however, that these conditions were caused when you were in control of the property, and he must also show the actual cost of repair. Sometimes landlords exaggerate these costs.

For a tenant to be successful in this type of action, it is important that the property rented be left in the same good order as it was when the rental period began. It is also important that you present the lease (if one exists) or any written correspondence between you and the landlord. Gather your receipt for the security deposit, together with any rental receipts or cancelled checks. If you believe a dispute may arise, take photographs before you leave, being certain that they are clear. You should itemize any damage to the property when you originally rented it, and list any damage that there may have been at the time you left.

If you are sued and you are the landlord, you should document the reason for not making payment to the tenant. Prepare a list of specific damages and the amount required to repair the damages, with actual receipts for any out-of-pocket expenses. If there is a question of serious damage, photographs should be taken showing the specific damage.

Harry Goldfarb and Bessie Goldfarb v. *Dogwood Manor*
CLAIM: Return of security deposit

Harry Goldfarb and his wife, Bessie, have been tenants of Dogwood Manor for eleven years. When they first moved in, the apartment building was new and they were required to pay a security deposit in the amount of $225, which at that time was the same as one month's rent. Upon their retirement, they decided not to renew their lease because they wanted to move to a warmer, sunnier climate. The landlord's agent, Ruth Prism, was called upon to make the final inspection so the Goldfarbs could be reimbursed for their entire security deposit plus interest for eleven years. Miss Prism told the Goldfarbs that they would receive a check for what was due them within a few days.

The tenants packed and were ready to move to Florida, but the landlord had not acted. Upon inquiry, they were told that they would not receive all of their security deposit back because the carpet had begun to show wear and they had left holes in the wall where paintings had hung.

Having learned about Small Claims Court at a senior citizens' meeting, Mr. Goldfarb immediately filed a Small Claims Court action against his landlord. The landlord was surprised, as he thought the Goldfarbs had left for Florida. He knew Mr. Goldfarb would be in a poor position to take action once he had gone out of town. At the time of the hearing (nineteen days after filing), not only did Mr. and Mrs. Goldfarb appear, but also they notified at least twenty other tenants, friends, and supporters, who also appeared. After Mr. Goldfarb presented his case, Miss Prism stood up and indicated in a very businesslike manner that the carpets had become somewhat worn and that the apartment needed painting. The judge inquired as to whether carpet should last for eleven years and further, whether an apartment should be painted as a matter of course by the landlord after eleven years. Unable to give a satisfactory response, she closed her file as the judge announced his verdict.

Only through the quick response of Small Claims Court was justice done in this matter, for if the Goldfarbs had moved to Florida without receiving their check, they would have had to come back to their community in order to prove their case. The faith that they and their many friends put in the system was justified.

Result: In the case of *Harry Goldfarb and Bessie Goldfarb v. Dogwood Manor,* the claimant was awarded the full amount of the security deposit together with interest for eleven years, and the court costs of this action. Interest in this case is required by state law from the time the security deposit is collected.

Although the case of *Harry Goldfarb and Bessie Goldfarb v. Dogwood Manor* was a relatively simple one, often the landlord-tenant disputes involve legal defenses, as in the case of *Sandy Tulley* v. *Sam Port,* which follows.

Sandy Tulley v. Sam Port
CLAIM: Return of security deposit
DEFENSE: Improper notice by tenant

Sandy Tulley rented one half of a house from Sam Port for about a year. Although she had no lease, Sandy and Sam had an oral agreement and she gave him the sum of $250 as security. She paid the monthly rent on time, except during the month when she had difficulty with leaky faucets, a toilet that would not work, and broken windows. During those months, when these items were not repaired at her request, she deducted money from the rent and had the work done herself. Mr. Port never complained.

The other half of Mr. Port's house had been unoccupied until the fall of the year, when Port, his wife, and three children moved in. A few days later, Sandy Tulley began noticing insects in her apartment. First, she saw an occasional roach walking around her kitchen. Then there were several roaches in the hallway. She called Port, whose wife, Thelma, said they had had the same problem in the last place they lived, adding that maybe they brought the roaches with them. She assured Sandy the problem would be taken care of.

As time passed, things got worse. Sam did not even make repairs that were required by the city property maintenance code. Sandy, feeling frustrated and angry, contacted a city inspector to inspect the rented property thoroughly. When the plumbing still went unrepaired and the roaches multiplied, Sandy packed up her bags and left. She said she was no longer going to live in Sam Port's house and demanded her security deposit back. Mr. Port said he would return it in a day or two.

When he did not return the deposit, Sandy contacted him. He told her, "If you want your money, hire a lawyer." Sandy brought this action to Small Claims Court. Sandy appeared at the hearing with her mother. Both were nervous but became more relaxed as Sandy told her story.

Sam's only defense was that Sandy did not comply with the law that requires a tenant give thirty days' notice before leaving. He said that because she did not give the notice, he was unable to rent the property immediately and he lost $250 in rent. Sandy's rent had been paid up to the date she left the property.

To substantiate her claim, Sandy had the court clerk issue a subpoena to Steve Miller, the building inspector. He stated at the hearing that he found seven property maintenance code violations. He added that he found several roaches running about the floors and walls.

When the judge asked how many roaches there were, he said, "Well, Judge, you could have divided them up into two groups and had a pretty good game of Capture the Flag."

The judge inquired, "In other words, do you believe that that apartment was not in livable condition and that Sandy Tulley was correct in leaving?"

The inspector answered, "Put it this way, Judge. If I had a small child living with me, I would probably have left faster than Miss Tully did."

Upon further questioning, the judge learned that roaches are difficult to exterminate. It appeared that they had arrived at the property with the landlord when he moved into the other half of the house. In his final statement, Mr. Port said that living with roaches is a part of renting. Renters, he added, should expect it.

Result: In the case of *Sandy Tully* v. *Sam Port,* the judge ruled for the tenant in the full amount of $250 plus court costs. This was a case in which a legal defense of improper notice was raised by the landlord. However, the property became uncomfortable and unlivable, due to actions of the landlord. Since nothing was immediately done to remedy the problem, the notice provision requiring Sandy to notify her landlord of her leaving would not apply.

The judge felt Sandy acted wisely in calling the city inspector to add credibility to her claim.

Landlord-Tenant Claims

Another situation occurs if you have given a cash deposit to a landlord in anticipation of renting a property, but have never moved in. You do not automatically lose that deposit. Each case is different, and it is necessary to consider the reasons for the deposit being given. Was it to reserve the property for the signing of a lease, or did it represent a normal security deposit, as in the Goldfarb case? If you decided not to move in just because you changed your mind, you may not have lost all of the deposit. The landlord has a duty to try to rerent the property. If it is rented for the time you said you were going to take it, then the landlord would be entitled to keep only that portion of your deposit for expenses he actually incurred in rerenting, such as advertisements, agent's fees, and any out-of-pocket expenses. If it was not rerented, you may lose the entire deposit.

On the other hand, there are those cases in which you give a deposit and agree to move in, but the landlord fails to live up to his promises as to the condition of the apartment.

Jack Frost prepared to move into an apartment with his family on the first of the month after giving the landlord a $200 security deposit. On the day he was ready to move, his landlord told him the old tenants had not yet left and that he should come back in a week. Mr. Frost said he no longer wanted the apartment if he had to wait a week. He brought his claim to Small Claims Court, not only for the $200 deposit return, but also for consequential damages, such as the hiring of a truck and the expense of housing his family in a hotel for three nights until he could find an alternate place to stay.

Deposits have also been returned when the landlord has not prepared the apartment as agreed at the time of the rental agreement. There are many other kinds of cases involving claims by tenants against landlords. Another common problem is a landlord's failure to supply services as provided in the lease. If a landlord, for an example, fails to supply heat or hot water as required, the tenant may be able to withhold rent. When the rent is withheld, the landlord will often start an eviction proceeding against the tenant. This ultimately may result in extensive court appearances by both parties.

Tom McGlynn, a tenant in a high-rise, had no heat for seven days. His prorata rent for the time when there was no heat was $70 (seven days at $10 per day). A clause in his lease stated that if the landlord failed to provide heat for more than three days, the tenant would not be responsible for rent for the cold days. An additional damage clause in the lease required the landlord to pay the sum of $10 per day as a penalty. Tom continued to pay the rent in full, but at the end of the month sent a notice to his landlord requesting a refund to him in the amount of $70 as a prorata rent and $70 as a damage penalty according to the lease. The landlord refused and Tom McGlynn brought an action in Small Claims Court for a total of $140. After viewing the lease, the judge ruled in favor of the tenant.

In this matter the tenant at no time raised any question of breaking the contract because he continued to pay rent. Instead he sought his remedy by first making a demand upon the landlord and then bringing an action in Small Claims Court. By doing this, the tenant avoided an eviction proceeding, even though the landlord may not have been successful. Tom McGlynn took the initiative on his ground—Small Claims Court.

There have been other actions brought by tenants against landlords in Small Claims Court, including failure to supply services such as trash collection or cleaning services. Small Claims Court opens many options to aid parties in complying with their written lease agreements.

In addition to the obligations stated in the lease, the landlord may not act negligently toward the tenant. For example, Julie Swan told her landlord that there was a leak coming from her ceiling. He made very inexpensive, temporary repairs instead of fixing the pipe properly. Julie had just completed some display work for her advertising job when suddenly the same pipe burst, spilling water all over her work and her newly re-covered chair.

The landlord's negligence resulted in Julie Swan's being paid not only for repair of the chair, but also for the consequential damages of the fair value of her labor in working on her art display.

For other negligence cases, see Chapter XI, which defines the liability of one party to the other.

Checklist for Tenant as Claimant

- Lease, if there is one.
- Receipt for security deposit and rental receipts or canceled checks.
- Photographs of the residence prior to the time of leaving.
- Checklist of any damage at the time the apartment was originally rented.
- Any witnesses who could substantiate your position (a friend who helped you move, for example).

Checklist for Landlord as Respondent

- List of specific damages, amounts required to repair, and actual receipts.
- Photographs of property showing damage.
- Have in court person who made inspections before and after rental period.

CLAIMS AGAINST TENANTS

Although people often think of a lease as protection for a tenant who may be treated unfairly by a landlord, the reverse is often seen in Small Claims Court. In many cases, it is the landlord who feels wronged by actions of the tenant.

Esther Rath v. Bobbie Washington
CLAIM: Landlord claim against tenant for damage

Esther Rath owned a two-family house and rented the first floor to Bobbie Washington and his family on a month-to-month basis. Mr. Washington did not have enough money for a security deposit, but he did have enough for the first month's rent of $250. Mrs. Rath accepted the rent and told him that he would have to keep the property in good condition. They inspected the apartment together. It had just been painted and decorated, and a new kitchen had been installed.

The arrangement worked well and Washington paid the rent on time for nearly a year and a half. He then gave Mrs. Rath proper notice that he was going to leave the property within thirty days, as he had purchased a new home. Mrs. Rath accepted the notice and said that at the time he was ready to leave, he should call her so that she could make an inspection of the property for damage.

On the last day, Washington attempted to contact Mrs. Rath, but she was not home, so he left the keys in her mailbox. The next day, Mrs. Rath found that the property was not in the same condition as when it was rented. Her inspection revealed that the apartment needed cleaning; it appeared it had not been vacuumed in several months. She also found a burn mark on the new counter in the kitchen, and many of the walls had small holes where pictures had hung. She took photographs of the kitchen counter and of the walls and hired a woman to clean.

She also called the man who installed the kitchen and he told her the burn mark would not come out of the counter. He said the damaged portion would have to be replaced for $102. Mrs. Rath found a person to spackle the 25 holes in the walls at $1.00 a hole. Although Mrs. Rath had expected to repaint after the tenants left, she did not expect to clean. The cleaning lady took a full day to clean the apartment and restore it to its original condition. She charged Mrs. Rath $35. Esther Rath contacted Bobbie Washington with regard to payment of the total sum, which was $162. He indicated that it was no longer his problem and that he didn't remember any of the damage.

Mrs. Rath filed this claim in Small Claims Court, and appeared together with a witness who inspected the property. She then presented the court with the photographs of the kitchen counter, the bill for the kitchen's installation at the beginning of the tenancy, and the bill for replacement of the countertop. She also produced a photograph of the walls showing the holes, and receipts itemizing costs from the cleaning lady and the painter.

Washington's only defense was that he did not remember the burn mark or how it got on the countertop and that holes in walls were normal in apartments. He felt if he paid $250 a month rent, he didn't have to clean the apartment.

Result: In the case of *Esther Rath* v. *Bobbie Washington,* decision was granted in full for the landlord, Esther Rath, in the amount of $162.

In this case, the landlord prepared her claim well. She presented photographs of the property to illustrate the damage. She documented a reasonable cost of repair and even presented a bill showing the cost of original construction. Showing reasonable repair costs is important. Sometimes a landlord will exaggerate the claim by charging outrageously high prices for repair of damage or replacement, adversely affecting credibility of the entire testimony. If the judge believes you are exaggerating the truth about any aspect of the case, the law permits him or her to discredit all of your testimony. It is important to be honest and fair.

Whether or not a landlord can collect for repainting depends on the length of tenancy. If, for example, a tenant was in the property for only two or three months and the newly painted walls were in very bad condition, the landlord would be entitled to a repainting allowance. If the tenancy is for a year or more, it is customary that the tenant not be charged for repainting, even if the walls are soiled. The tenant should check with the landlord to see whether permission is required for hanging pictures and what the liability will be.

If a tenant is still living in the leased property and owes rent to the landlord, an action may be commenced in the regular term of court or in Housing Court to evict the tenant and obtain the rent due. In the event the landlord does not wish to evict a tenant who still owes rent, or if the tenant has left the property owing the rent, the Small Claims Court option is available. Small Claims Court is used by landlords to bring action to collect rent due, particularly against former tenants who left owing rent. In a furnished apartment a tenant sometimes takes some of the furniture when he or she leaves. A landlord then may bring an action against the former tenant for a reasonable value of the furniture that was removed.

The cases illustrate that Small Claims Court can be used by the landlord as well as the tenant to settle most disputes involving a sum of money.

Checklist for Landlord as Claimant

- Inspection checklist of any damage before tenant occupies property.
- Any bills showing pertinent work done before tenancy.
- Photographs of property where damage exists.
- Estimates to repair property.
- Any witnesses who viewed the property with the landlord after tenancy.
- Receipts for any payments made.
- Be prepared to justify that your charges are reasonable (use expert witness or bring to court at least two comparable estimates of repair).

Checklist for Tenant as Respondent

- Photographs of the property.
- Witnesses to show there was no damage (this is often someone who helped you move out).

CHAPTER

IX

Defective Goods and Merchandise

How many times have you purchased an item that, after a period of time, you learned was not fit for the purpose you intended it? Perhaps you were lured into purchasing it by a salesperson or advertisement. When you paid your money, you thought you were purchasing a good product that you could use for a specific purpose. A short time later, the product fails and you are disappointed. Perhaps you take the item back (if it is one that can be taken back) and ask for replacement or repair. If you do not get satisfaction, the alternative is Small Claims Court.

Some items of defective merchandise cannot be returned because their use results in the item's being consumed, such as house paint. In this case, you can attempt to obtain a reimbursement from the person or company that sold you the item. Once again, if you are not satisfied, take the matter to Small Claims Court. You, as the consumer, should not turn around and say, "Well, I guess I'll just forget about it and never buy another item from this company or person." But you'll probably feel better if you go through the procedure and right the wrong!

It is important in the preparation of your defective-goods

case that you bring your original sales receipt to court. Also, if the price of the item has gone up since you purchased it, you should obtain an advertisement, brochure, or another estimate from a reputable dealer as to the replacement value of your item. If repair alone is sufficient to restore the item to good working order, you should obtain an estimate of repair. Witnesses could be helpful if they were with you when you purchased the item and heard what representations were made to you that were not lived up to. Also bring any advertisements, brochures, or articles that show that the item was misrepresented. Most importantly, you should preserve the item that is the subject of the lawsuit and bring it to court.

If you are being sued, you should obtain any documents concerning the item and any manufacturer's literature to show what the item should or could do. If you feel the item was defective because the claimant may have abused the product, you may point this out and highlight in your literature a statement that it is not guaranteed against abuse other than the ordinary use for which it was intended. The person who was actually involved in the transaction with the claimant should be present for the respondent in Small Claims Court. In cases in which a store manager appears in court without any detailed knowledge except records of the transaction, the defense is incomplete. You should have a new sample of the original product available for the court to see.

Betty Sherwood v. *Longer Nails, Inc.*
CLAIM: Defective beauty product

Longer Nails, Inc., is a company that advertises that it meets the needs of women who desire longer fingernails without waiting for them to grow. Betty Sherwood had always wanted longer nails, but in her profession as a secretary, she was unable to grow them. The week before her daughter's wedding, she decided to

Defective Goods and Merchandise

pamper herself and go to Longer Nails, Inc., to have fingernails placed on her fingers for the wedding so that she would be appropriately "dressed." A few days before the wedding, she went to Longer Nails, Inc., and had the plastic nails applied and polished in a color that matched her dress. The nails cost $20. Betty was told by the operator that the nails were strong, they would not chip or break, and they would last at least four weeks. When her own nails began to grow in several weeks, Longer Nails would gently fall off.

Two days after the application, on the day of the wedding, Betty's nails began to crack, flake, and fall apart. She tried to remove the Longer Nails but the glue held fast. At her daughter's wedding, Betty was stuck with Longer Nails that looked awful. Betty and her sister performed a last-minute repair job using nail cutters and polish, which did help the nails look presentable.

Annoyed and upset with the fact that Longer Nails, Inc., had failed her, Betty brought a claim in Small Claims Court for the $20 plus tax. She appeared in court, bringing one of her fingernails that was placed on by Longer Nails, Inc. Longer Nails was represented by the company president and chief operator, Marie Veruso. After Betty stated her case, Miss Veruso became extremely irate and said that her company's product was perfect. "It is impossible to chip or crack our nails. The only way Longer Nails can be damaged is with a hammer," she said. Betty Sherwood became upset that Marie Veruso had falsely insinuated that she had either banged a hammer on her nails or was telling a lie. The judge then told the ladies to calm down or neither of them would win. The court attendant stepped forward giving a stern look to each of the women. Order was restored. The judge had no reason to doubt the word of either woman. He was convinced that Longer Nails was probably a very good product that just didn't work when applied to Betty Sherwood. He reasoned that they might have been affected by the weather conditions at the time, or that they just would not take to Betty's fingers. Both parties claimed it was a matter of principle. But the court relied on the law that the product was not as described and was not fit for the purpose.

Result: In the case of *Betty Sherwood* v. *Longer Nails, Inc.,* the judge awarded in favor of the claimant $20 plus tax, plus court costs. (During the proceeding, the claimant indicated that the name of the respondent should be changed from Longer Nails, Inc., to Nails No Longer, Inc.)

Rocco's Five O'Clock Club v. *Manny Haber*
CLAIM: Defective floor covering

Manny Haber often dined at Rocco's Five O'Clock Club. One evening he and the proprietor, Rocco Mingo, had a discussion about the fact that a new carpet for the club would be very nice. Manny, who was in the floor-covering business, told Mingo that he would make him a terrific deal on a new type of carpet tile. Manny assured Mingo that the tiles would look very plush in the elegant eatery. Rocco wasn't sure about doing business with Manny, but Manny's sales pitch sounded good and Manny was a regular customer of his. He decided that he would go for the $525 and have the floor tiles of carpet installed. Manny Haber told Mingo that these tiles were put down in one-by-two-foot sections and would last a lifetime. They would be durable, washable, and their self-adhesive backing would stick to the floor forever.

Several weeks after installation, Mingo noticed that after normal shampooing of the carpet, the tiles were sliding around and some were actually coming up. Manny responded that this was impossible and could not happen to his product. Mingo demanded a replacement floor covering. Manny refused.

On the day of the hearing, Manny arrived in court with a one-by-two-foot red floor tile that had marks of dirt and discoloration. As Manny and Mingo were led in by the Court attendant, Mingo said, in a loud voice, "I want him [pointing

Defective Goods and Merchandise

to Manny] arrested."

The judge said, "This is not Criminal Court, this is Small Claims Court."

"But he stole my piece of carpet last night and I want him arrested," Mingo shouted. Mingo and his brothers, "Blue Boy" and "Knee High," glared at poor Manny Haber. Two court attendants and the judge restored order.

After Rocco Mingo accused Manny of stealing the tiles and stated his claim that the tiles were not as suited or represented by Manny, Manny told the court that he had borrowed the tile from the floor of the restaurant to show how greasy it was. Manny said that, in fact, Rocco's Five O'Clock Club had the greasiest kitchen floor in all of the city and that each time a cart was rolled from the kitchen into the dining area, the grease would come with it. He said that the grease seeping underneath the tiles caused the carpet squares to move around. Mingo retorted that this was not true, that his kitchen is clean, and that the grease in his club is ordinary. At this point, had Manny Haber stopped talking, he might have won and the claim would have been dismissed.

But as the men became more tense, Manny tried harder to prove his point. He went too far when he said, "This carpet does not in any way move or slide. It will stick forever." He then took a new piece of tile to prove to the court what a good product he had. He threw it down on a linoleum tile floor in front of the judge. "Judge," he said, "I believe in this so much that if you can make this tile move even an inch, I'll give you a hundred dollars!" He punctuated his exclamation by kicking the rug to show that it wouldn't slide. The carpet slid two feet across the linoleum floor.

Manny Haber overpowered his case. He should have known when to sit down and not say any more. As the judge excused all parties, Rocco Mingo said, "Where do I file my charge for larceny? This man stole my carpet."

Result: In the case of *Rocco's Five O'Clock Club* v. *Manny*

Haber, judgment was awarded to Rocco Mingo in the amount of $525 plus court costs. It was apparent to the judge that Manny had misrepresented the carpet, which was not of the type that was required in a restaurant (or in a courtroom, for that matter).

John Chapin and Judy Chapin v. The Gold Shaft
CLAIM: Defective jewelry

John Chapin went to a local jewelry store known as The Gold Shaft and purchased a magnificent 14k gold rope bracelet to surprise his wife for their tenth anniversary. The bracelet cost $370. His wife, Judy, was delighted with the gift. The bracelet was a little bit too big, however, so Judy and John returned to the store to see if it could be made smaller. Josephine Winston, the proprietor of the store, said that there would be no problem and measured Judy's wrist with a special tape. Mrs. Winston then had the bracelet shortened to size 6-¾", relying on her own measurement of Judy's wrist.

When the bracelet came back from being sized, it was much too tight. The Chapins were disappointed. Mrs. Winston assured them that she could have it lengthened to size 7 because she saved the pieces. The Chapins balked, indicating that they did not wish to have a bracelet that had been shortened and then lengthened. They felt they would always be able to tell that it was a repaired bracelet, not in its original condition. They demanded their money back. Mrs. Winston refused, saying they would not be able to tell where the modification was made. She shipped the bracelet to a jewelry repair shop to be adjusted.

John and Judy Chapin brought this action to recover their $370, saying that the merchandise they purchased was not in its original state of quality.

At the time of the trial, Josephine Winston produced the bracelet, claiming that it looked just like new. The court asked

Defective Goods and Merchandise

that she produce one that had not been altered so that a comparison could be made. The Chapins pointed out that near the clasp, where the bracelet had been lengthened, the gold was not pliable and loose, but in fact was stiffened because of the necessary soldering.

The judge asked several questions of both parties. He learned that the proprietor of The Gold Shaft, Miss Winston, had made the mistake because of inexperience. It was the first time that she had measured anybody's wrist. The judge believed that the Chapins intended to purchase a new bracelet, not the one that was modified as a result of Miss Winston's error.

Although the flaw may not have been readily detectable to the salesperson, the judge believed that Mrs. Chapin should not have to wear a bracelet that was less perfect than her husband originally intended.

Result: In the case of *John Chapin and Judy Chapin v. The Gold Shaft,* the judge ruled that the claimant would receive the full award of $370 plus tax, court costs, and interest from date of the sale. The Gold Shaft would keep the bracelet.

Checklist for Claimant

- Original sales slip or contract.
- Estimate of cost for a replacement or repair of product.
- Any literature or advertisement you relied upon.
- The product or subject of the claim.
- Any witnesses to substantiate the facts.

Checklist for Respondent

- Original sales slip or contract.
- Manufacturer's warranty and disclaimer form (in case of abuse).
- Salesperson who sold the product.

Carol Burke v. Connie Cook
CLAIM: Request refund of money for defective automobile

Connie Cook advertised in the local paper to sell an eight-year-old foreign car with seventy-five thousand miles on it. On the first morning after the ad appeared, Carol Burke called and asked about the car. Connie told her that it was a one-owner vehicle that had been well maintained; it had a good heater; and it would make a good second car. Carol was also told that equipment on the car included snow tires, an FM radio, bucket seats, and an inside hood release. Connie said she would accept $300 in cash for the automobile.

Ms. Burke was very interested in the car, although she had only $300 to spend on a car and knew it was hard to find one at that price that could pass inspection. Connie and Ms. Burke arranged a meeting. When Ms. Burke saw the car, she noted it was rusted badly, but after she drove it around the block, she felt it would meet her needs. She didn't care how it looked as long as it gave her good and safe transportation. Connie assured her that everything she had been told was true, but that she would have to accept the vehicle in "as is" condition. In the law this means the buyer must accept whatever defects there are.

Carol Burke agreed, saying she didn't care how bad the vehicle looked as long as it passed state inspection.

Connie Cook then wrote on the bill of sale, "Will pass inspection when body is repaired (left front fender). Also, state inspection will require the left front side light to be replaced." With that, arrangements were made for Ms. Burke to pick up the car and pay the total of $300 cash. As Carol drove the vehicle away from Connie's residence, Carol noticed she had a great deal of difficulty in steering the automobile. She decided to take it to her mechanic to have it adjusted, but was frightened driving any farther, so she pulled over to the side of the road and called for a tow truck to take it to the garage.

Defective Goods and Merchandise

The next day she spoke with Scott Armstrong, the chief mechanic, who told her he could not fix the steering because the frame of the automobile was completely severed behind the cross member on the left side and the frame was rusted through both sides. The car was worthless. Ms. Burke was angry. She thought she would be out the entire $300 because she purchased this automobile "as is." Then she remembered that Connie Cook had promised that the car would pass state inspection with minor repairs to the left front fender and front side light. She asked Scott if it would pass state inspection and he said he would run through the tests and advise her.

Later that day, Scott told her there were seven additional violations and that the car was completely unsafe to drive. It was simply too old to be repaired.

Carol Burke then called Connie Cook and told her of the situation and Connie said, "Well, I didn't know about those defects, but why don't you try to sell it for junk?" Carol Burke's response was a trip to the local Small Claims Court. In court, both the claimant and the respondent came forward together. With them was the respondent's mechanic, who had inspected the vehicle eight months before.

Miss Burke related the incident and said that in addition to getting her $300 back, she was requesting another $87 for consequential damages, including $21 for tax she had to pay the Motor Vehicle Department at the time she registered the car; a registration fee of $26 to the state; an inspection fee of $6; and other costs of inconvenience.

She also brought a certified statement from the mechanic who decided not to pass the vehicle through the state inspection, stating why the vehicle had failed. This type of statement is often permitted in Small Claims Court when it is on the proper form, obtained from the court clerk.

Miss Cook's mechanic, who had inspected the vehicle eight months before, testified that he had passed it, but really didn't remember much about the car.

Miss Cook further stated that Ms. Burke had the obligation to try to sell the car and get whatever money she could for it.

Result: In the case of *Carol Burke* v. *Connie Cook,* the judge found in favor of the claimant in the full amount of $300, the purchase price of the car, together with the consequential damages of $21 for the tax paid to the state, and the state inspection of $6.00. He did not award her the $26 registration fee because that could be transferred to another vehicle that Ms. Burke might purchase.

In this case, the seller did show the vehicle properly, did not know of the defect, and sold it in "as is" condition. Usually, this would relieve her of any liability from future claims no matter what condition of the car. She made her mistake, however, by adding an exception to the "as is" by guaranteeing that the car would pass inspection. It was obvious from the statement by the claimant's mechanic that it could not be driven safely and would never pass inspection. Although the respondent brought a mechanic into court, his testimony was ineffectual, as his inspection occurred some eight months before and much could have happened in the interim. Additionally, his recollection was vague.

This was an unusual case in that a certified statement by a mechanic was better proof than that of an actual witness.

Problems with car mechanics are not unusual in Small Claims Court, as you will see in Chapter X. Be careful in choosing a mechanic or you may end up in court like Sara Simon (see *Sara Simon* v. *Bumper's Corner Service* in Chapter X).

CHECKLIST FOR CLAIMANT

- Copy of advertisement, if any.
- Original bill of sale or receipt from seller.
- Canceled check or other form showing payment.

Defective Goods and Merchandise 101

- Any document showing a represenation made by seller that you relied on.
- Any bills you incurred as a result of the product being defective.
- Certified statement of mechanic or testimony from mechanic in court.

CHECKLIST FOR RESPONDENT

- Any advertisement showing condition of car.
- Receipts showing repairs you had made to the car prior to sale.
- Proof of last official state inspection.
- Any witnesses present at the time of the transaction.
- Prices of other comparable automobiles sold for in area (especially helpful if you sold the car for a much lower price than the prevailing rate).

DEFECTIVE PRODUCT—GOOD-FAITH RESPONDENT

You may be upset and frustrated that a certain product does not work properly or is defective. You have taken it back to the salesperson a couple of times and each time he has tried to remedy the situation by either repair or replacement of the product. You find that the repair is insufficient and the new product is also defective. Eventually you may merely wish to have your money back. If the salesperson refuses, you return the product and bring a claim in Small Claims Court for the full purchase price of the product.

This type of case is one in which the respondent shows good faith all along. From the time you complain until the time you serve your claim, he or she has attempted to right the wrong but, for some reason, has been unable to. At the time of the court appearance, the respondent may bring in another product, which is not defective. If you, as the claimant, are not satisfied, the judge will make a determination and either order that you have your money refunded or order you to take the new product. If you cannot determine whether the replacement works until you use it a few times, the judge may adjourn the case for a few weeks. If he does not hear from you, he will assume that the case is settled. If you find that the replacement is also unsatisfactory, you should inform the court. The judge will then direct you to return the product and tell the respondent to pay you a full refund. Or he might direct a rehearing of the case, depending on the specific circumstances.

Anita Dickson v. Ben Klaver
CLAIM: Defective silverware

The respondent, Ben Klaver, who is a friend of the claimant, sold silverware door-to-door. During an evening of family socializing, the respondent suggested that perhaps Mrs. Dickson would like to purchase eight full five-piece place settings of stainless-steel dinnerware. Mrs. Dickson believed it would be a lovely gift for her nine-year-old daughter to keep over the years as an investment, and perhaps use in the future for her own family. The child, herself, proudly picked out the pattern and became very excited about the prospect of having her own chest of dinnerware.

After several weeks, the silver arrived and Mrs. Dickson paid the full amount of $130 for the set and the silver chest. She put all of the silverware in the chest and put it away for several weeks. While she was planning Thanksgiving dinner, Mrs. Dickson decided it would be nice to use the silverware. When she took it out of the chest, she discovered that the seams on all the knives were imperfect and did not match. She and her child were quite disappointed and contacted the respondent. Mr. Klaver agreed that they did not look proper and sent them back to the manufacturer. In a few weeks, Mrs. Dickson received eight new knives. Once again, she was not satisfied with the

Defective Goods and Merchandise

seams and gave Mr. Klaver the entire silverware set back. She then brought an action in Small Claims Court, seeking a refund of her money, less the price of the silverchest, which she wished to keep.

When Mrs. Dickson came into court, she told her story and presented the canceled check. She requested a refund in full because the silver was not satisfactory and was certainly not as represented by the salesman, Mr. Klaver.

While Mr. Klaver agreed that some of the pieces of silverware were imperfect, he agreed to stand by and guarantee replacement without charge, which was the company's policy. In fact, Mr. Klaver brought to court a factory-fresh set of stainless silverware, all forty-two pieces still wrapped. He told the judge that he wanted to keep the sale and he would be glad to give Mrs. Dickson the new set, which she could inspect, piece by piece, in court. Mrs. Dickson expressed doubt whether the silverware would be proper and didn't even know if she wanted it anymore because of her bad experience with the other two shipments. Mr. Klaver said he had done everything possible to comply with the guarantee and would continue to do so if this product were not to Mrs. Dickson's satisfaction.

At the request of the judge, all forty-two pieces, one by one, were unwrapped and inspected for defects by the judge and both parties. The claimant indicated that the goods looked much better than the other shipments, but she did not know if she wanted them. When Mr. Klaver indicated to her that the price of a set had increased over the last several months by $75, and showed a brochure to prove it, Mrs. Dickson changed her mind and agreed to accept the unblemished third shipment.

It was apparent that both parties had prepared their cases well. Mrs. Dickson documented her claim and presented her canceled check and a witness to testify about the imperfect silver. Mr. Klaver brought forth brochures, showed what the silver should look like, and testified as to his attempts to resolve the problem. He also prepared himself in the best possible way by bringing a fresh set into court.

In this case, the judge did not make a decision; rather, he aided the parties in making their own decision. At the conclusion of the case, both parties left, Mrs. Dickson with the silverware, and Mr. Klaver with his sale. All appeared satisfied. A judge, too, has a feeling of well-being when justice is done by the Small Claims Court procedure!

Result: In the case of *Anita Dickson* v. *Ben Klaver,* settled by the parties.

In this type of case in which the respondent shows good faith, he is accomplishing two purposes: By showing good will he may keep this customer for a future transaction; and he is also saving the profit he made on the original transaction. Since the respondent is in business to serve customers and make money, he fulfilled both goals by his actions.

You have already read another example of this type of claim in Chapter IV in the case involving the improper repair of a television set. In that case, you'll recall, the owner of the set merely wanted his set repaired properly. The repairman, although he was sued for the full value of the set, was truly interested in making the proper repair. After the court appearance, he showed good faith, and both parties received what they wanted. The owner of the television got a television that was in working order, and the repairman saved his profit.

It might be added that within two weeks after both of these cases were concluded, three of the four parties sent letters to the judge thanking him for giving them the opportunity to right their wrongs without the necessity of a money award.

DEFECTIVE PRODUCT RESULTING IN CONSEQUENTIAL DAMAGES

You have invested money in a new product that you later learn is defective. Hopefully, the product can be returned or

Defective Goods and Merchandise

exchanged for a new one. At times, however, a defective product will result in additional damages to you. This is called consequential damages or those that result from another defect.

An extreme example of this is a short in an electrical appliance causing a house to burn down. You would be entitled to return or replacement of the electrical appliance, but also the party who manufactured or sold the appliance may be responsible for all of the resulting damage. A more common type of problem existed for the Tillman Family.

Chester Tillman and Betty Tillman
v.
Bill's Appliance Center
CLAIM: Defective refrigerator and spoiled food

Chester and Betty Tillman and their three children live together with Chester's brother, his wife, and five children. All were sharing one refrigerator. The food for this many people was a bit much for the refrigerator, so the families decided to go to Bill's Appliance Center to look for a second refrigerator.

They looked at several new refrigerators, but were unable to afford them, so Bill Quick, the owner of Bill's Appliance Center, showed them a used but "good and reliable" two-door refrigerator. When asked if it would last a long time, Bill said he "would stand by the quality and reliability of the unit."

The Tillmans paid for it, including the $7.00 delivery charge, and it was set up in their home on July 3. On July 4, the Tillmans noticed that the unit was not cooling and that some of the food they had placed in it had begun to spoil. The chicken, in fact, was turning green.

Betty Tillman drove over to Bill's Appliance Center and found it closed. She then went to Bill's home and told him that the unit was not operating. He said he would be over later to repair it. When he didn't come later in the day, she once again called him and he said he was having trouble with his truck but would probably be there the next day, which was Saturday, July 5. She became upset, but said she would wait one more day.

On Saturday, after Bill did not appear to repair it, Betty called and asked him where he was. Bill indicated that it was a weekend and that his truck was broken down.

She said, "Well, I'll come over and get you and drive you to my house."

Bill's retort was, "Do you work on Saturday and Sunday too?" and he refused to make the repair.

Several days later the Tillmans filed their claim in Small Claims Court for return of the money in full. At the hearing, each side told its story. Bill admitted that he said he would stand behind the unit, but stated he felt it was working okay, once he didn't hear from them after his refusal to come on the weekend.

Result: In the case of *Chester Tillman and Betty Tillman* v. *Bill's Appliance Center,* the judge decided in favor of the Tillmans and against Bill's Appliance Center for the full amount and required the respondent to pick up the refrigerator at his own cost from the Tillman's home.

In addition to the full sum of $125 being awarded to the Tillmans, the judge awarded an additional $18.73 for spoiled food. The Tillmans supplied him with a grocery list as proof of what they lost. The judge felt that as a result of the inadequate response of the respondent, the claimants suffered the additional damage of spoiled poultry and dairy products.

It also should be noted that the judge decided that even though Bill did not want to make his repair on July 4, Saturday, or Sunday, people's needs continue and refrigerators don't select only weekdays between nine and five to break down. The judge believed that the seller had an obligation to make good on his word immediately, regardless of what time the event occurred, even though it wasn't at his convenience.

In this case, from the time of the sale until the time of the

Defective Goods and Merchandise

hearing in court, less than five weeks elapsed. This is an illustration of how quickly the Small Claims Court process can remedy an unfair situation.

One type of consequential damage is that which may occur as the result of a defective product, such as in the Tillman refrigerator case; another type involves expenses that a person might reasonably expect to incur as the result of the defective product or improper act of the respondent. Such was the situation with Richard Gardner.

Gardner had just purchased a new foreign car, which he drove 120 miles to a wedding reception. The car performed well on the first leg of the trip. The trip home was another matter. He had traveled only 5 miles toward home when the car suddenly lurched forward, started racing, and in his words, "took off." He had been driving on an expressway at 55 mph, and before he knew it the car was doing 95 mph. Suddenly, he related, there was a loud bang and the car slowed to a dead stop. Gardner had several choices at that point. He could stay overnight in a hotel and wait for his dealer to open the next morning so that he could call for advice, or he could call a tow truck to tow him and his family back home. He chose the latter because his was a rare kind of automobile and the only reputable dealer was in his home area. The tow bill came to $175 for a 115-mile trip.

The dealer agreed to repair the automobile, but refused to pay the tow bill. The court decided in favor of Mr. Gardner, as the towing was a consequential expense for damage from the original defective product. If Richard Gardner or his family had been injured as the result of the defective product, additional consequential damages would have resulted. Fortunately, he was an experienced high-speed driver because he had several years' training as a police officer. Because of Gardner's ability, the damages were kept to a minimum.

If you are involved in a situation that requires long-distance phone calls, keep track of them. They may also be recoverable as a consequential damage. For example, if the warranty on the product says, "Do not call your local dealer—contact the manufacturer," you may have to call out of town. If you get no satisfaction, you may bring an action against the local dealer and tack on as a damage the phone-call expense.

Lost wages directly incurred as the result of the negligence or the act of the respondent may also be recoverable in Small Claims Court. For example, if Richard Gardner had no way of getting to his job and as a result lost a day's pay, he may have been able to collect lost wages. Remember, however, that the time lost from work while you bring a claim to court and such related expenses as parking and mileage are not recoverable as damages.

There are many situations that might result in a consequential damage. The general rule is to determine whether or not there was a generally foreseeable and actual expense incurred as the result of the original defective product or wrongful act.

DEFECTIVE PRODUCT—IMPROPER INSTALLATION

Most products that we buy can be taken from the store or delivered to our home and used without anything further being done, but some items require installation. When you buy locks from a locksmith, you also buy the service of the locksmith installing them. The locks could be of fine quality, but if the installation is improper, you can bring action against the locksmith for any damages that were suffered as a result of the improper installation. This is what happened to Dianna Travers.

Dianna's Dairy Bar
v.
Carley's 24-Hour We Never Sleep Burglar Alarm Company

CLAIM: Inoperable burglar alarm

Dianna Travers owned and operated a dairy bar in a neighborhood that was recently plagued by frequent burglaries. Her store had been broken into twice in the past month. After a great deal of thought, she made a decision to call Carley Fouse, who operated Carley's 24-Hour We Never Sleep Burglar Alarm Company. Carley arrived promptly and explained to Dianna how he would make certain that she'd never have another break-in. His burglar alarm system was foolproof, and if anybody tried to gain entry to her store, the police would automatically be called and arrive on the scene to scare off the intruders.

Dianna did not inquire as to how the system would be installed, but after being assured by Carley that it would be 100 percent accurate, she signed a contract for $900 for the system's installation and gave Carley half in advance.

The system was promptly installed. Two days later, Dianna arrived at her place of business at five-thirty in the morning so she could get ready for her early customers. She noticed that the door had been forced open, glass was broken inside, her cash register had money taken from it, and her one electronic game machine, which produced big income for her, had been shattered.

Dianna became very upset, as she had relied upon the burglar alarm to ward off any difficulties. She refused to pay Carley the additional $450. Carley brought an action against Dianna in Small Claims Court to recover the $450.

At first, Carley made a simple presentation, saying he installed the system, had received half the money, and upon completion did not receive the other half.

The judge then turned to Dianna and said, "Well, why didn't you pay for it?"

She related the story about the burglary that occurred two days later. She also had done a great deal of homework and brought an expert with her, a person who had reinstalled the system properly.

The judge learned that Carley's electrician, instead of wiring the automatic dialer to the private phone, had wired it to a public pay phone in the restaurant. For it to work properly, the burglar, once he had broken into the restaurant, would have had to insert a dime in the pay phone so that the police would be alerted to his presence.

It became apparent to the judge that this was a case of an improper installation. Dianna desired to keep the system, now that she had had it properly hooked up for the sum of $35. She brought additional proof to show that her damage by theft far exceeded the $450 claim by Carley.

Result: In the case of *Dianna's Dairy Bar* v. *Carley's 24-Hour We Never Sleep Burglar Alarm Company,* the court found that Dianna owed nothing further and could keep the system. It might be added that the electrician who installed the system could not find a private phone line as required, so his boss told him that he should hook it up to the pay phone because Dianna would never know the difference. He was only interested in getting his money and did not care about performing a proper service.

Dianna remarked on the way out that it was appropriate that Carley own Carley's 24-Hour We Never Sleep Burglar Alarm Company because if she ran her business in the same manner that he ran his, she wouldn't be able to sleep nights either.

In this case, Miss Travers could have sued in a counterclaim for the damages she incurred in the burglary because this was a consequential damage not unlike that in *Chester Tillman and Betty Tillman* v. *Bill's Appliance Center* (defective refrigerator and spoiled food).

Defective Goods and Merchandise

Any case in which there has been improper installation of a product may be the subject of an action in Small Claims Court. The installation of wall-to-wall carpet is a subject that often comes up in Small Claims Court. The people who sell carpet often subcontract with different crews to do their work. Sometimes the carpet has either been cut too short or the seam is placed incorrectly. Most retailers will cooperate and right the wrong without the necessity of a suit in Small Claims Court, but the alternative is available.

Another case commonly heard involves automatic garage door openers. Although these are popular because of the convenience and security they offer, sometimes the programming is improper, causing the radio-activated device to open other people's garage doors. This faulty programming of the product is considered improper installation.

CHAPTER

X

Services Performed

THE PERFORMANCE OF services differs greatly from the sale or installation of a product. Before you purchase a product, you can look at it, touch it, try it out, have it demonstrated for you, choose among many types, and then decide if it's exactly as you want. Once the decision is made, you can pay for it, and if it doesn't work as agreed or as represented, you can return it and usually get your money back. Perhaps somebody else will buy it, if it's more suited for them.

Personal services are not tangible. You can't see in advance what someone promises to do for you. You and the person who is about to perform the services can discuss what you each have in mind and come to an agreement, either oral or written. He or she can show you the products of past service. The services performed for you are unique for each particular situation. Even if you have a specific set of plans such as blueprints for constructing a house or building a chimney, each item is to be placed in its proper order by the person who is performing the service. The only variables are the quality and care of the service. The evaluation of the performance is subjective. Only you can decide how you feel about the quality of service.

Services Performed 113

Many cases arise in Small Claims Court in which there is a dispute as to the performance of a service. Unlike a product, you cannot return the service. This chapter deals with the performance of improper services, as well as those that were properly performed and not paid for.

If you have ever left a product for service and the repairperson has gone beyond your authorization or even performed unnecessary repairs to your product, you will quickly understand the plights of Ned Benson, Chris Owens, and Sara Simons, whose cases appear in this Chapter. You may also wish to follow them to Small Claims Court.

IMPROPER SERVICES PERFORMED

Disputes arise when the result is not as anticipated. It is important that you tell the person who is performing the service specifically what you would like done. It might also be a good idea to do so in writing or with a sketch. If the service is not performed exactly as you had envisioned, your dissatisfaction can be remedied in an action in Small Claims Court.

In this type of case, each party will have to explain to the judge how he or she understood the agreement for repair. These cases usually arise when there is not a clear understanding between the parties about the repair. It is important for each side to present any witnesses who were present when the item was brought in for repair. The judge can be helped to reach a decision by seeing the item in dispute. People involved in this type of case are often very emotional, so it is important to be as calm as possible to avoid clouding the facts.

When you present a case such as this, you should have the original sales slip of the item or some proof of what the replacement cost would be and the receipt or repair slip from the person who was to do the work. If it's at all possible, bring the item so that the judge may see evidence of the improper work.

If you have any photographs to represent the item before the repair was done, they should be brought to court as well.

If you are sued, any literature dealing with the type of repair that is accepted in the trade should be brought to court along with any receipts or documents such as sketches, drawings, or notes given by the person suing you. If you have any item that is comparable to the subject of the repair, you should bring it to court, too.

Felicia Fillman v. *Angelo's Tailor Shop*
CLAIM: Improper dress alteration

Felicia Fillman purchased a beautiful long orange chiffon gown to wear for her daughter's wedding. It was a very expensive garment, costing more than $450. She wore it once. After her daughter's wedding, she took it to Angelo's Tailor Shop to be altered so that she could wear it as a street-length dress for other occasions. When Mrs. Fillman came to pick up the dress, the seamstress asked if she would try it on to see how it looked. Felicia said she didn't have the time, was sure it was fine, took the dress, and walked out of the store.

When she arrived home, she tried the dress on and found that the hem was uneven. The dress, according to her, was ruined for good. She brought this action to recover the full value of the dress.

At the time of trial, Felicia Fillman appeared as a robust, angry woman who was quite loud in pursuing her claim. She implied that the awful tailor and his seamstress ruined the dress and added that her memories of her daughter's wedding had been tarnished because the dress had been ruined.

Angelo testified that when the claimant brought the gown to his store, he had advised her that it would be very difficult to shorten a dress made of chiffon. He also told her that she would have to try the dress on so that he could measure it. He said she held it up to herself and said, "I want you to shorten it to

Services Performed 115

right here," pointing to below her knee. "I don't want to try it on in front of you." He noted that his customers usually tried on the clothes they wanted altered and said that it would be very difficult for him to do the alteration properly without a fitting. He told her he would try, but would make no guarantees about the result. When she came back into the store to pick up the dress, he said she had again been asked to try it on, and again she refused, saying, "I will take it just the way it is." She paid him $60 for the work and left.

Emotions were strong on both sides. Mrs. Fillman could not separate the ruined dress from her memories of her daughter's wedding, and the tailor's pride was on the line because he believed his professional reputation was at stake.

In deciding this case, the judge had to think about the purpose for which the dress was purchased. He decided it was really purchased for the daughter's wedding, a one-time use. If it was going to be worn again, a depreciation factor would have to be taken into consideration. Mrs. Fillman's failure to try on the dress in the shop both before and after it was altered was a determining factor in the case, suggesting that she accepted the work as offered. She created the problem herself.

Result: In the case of *Felicia Fillman* v. *Angelo's Tailor Shop,* the court awarded the sum of $60 to cover the repair bill. Any damage to the dress was not recoverable because of (1) the purpose for which the dress was intended initially; and (2) the claimant's own acts at the tailor shop through which she assumed the risk and accepted the work.

Sandra Pelcher v. *Billy Simpson's Shoe Repair*
CLAIM: Improper dyeing of leather boots

Sandra Pelcher talked her mother into buying her a pair of light tan boots for $75. Sometime later, for her high-school graduation, she was given a medium-color tan handbag. She wanted the boots dyed to match the handbag, which would complement an outfit she had. Sandra took the boots to a neighborhood shoe repairman, Billy Simpson, and told him she would like them dyed. He asked her what color she would like them dyed and she pointed to a pair of dark brown boots in the store and said she would like them two shades lighter. Billy said, "I don't know what you mean by 'two shades,'" and Sandra again pointed to the dark boots, and said, "You know what you're doing. Just make them lighter than those boots." Several days later Sandra and her mother entered the store to pick up the boots. Billy handed them over and charged $12 for the dye job. Both of the women became hysterical. Billy had dyed the boots dark brown. Sandra then filed a claim in Small Claims Court for the $75 value of the boots. She brought the boots and the handbag with her.

It was obvious that the handbag was a medium tan and the boots were very dark brown. Sandra told the judge that the boots were brand new, had never been worn, and that they were ruined because she couldn't wear them with her new handbag. Billy, on the other hand, indicated that she had never brought the handbag into the store to have the color matched, and, further, that when a piece of leather is dyed, there can be "no guarantee of how it comes out." Billy further said that he told Sandra this in the store. She admitted that she did not bring the handbag to be matched, but placed all of her faith in the expertise of Billy Simpson's Shoe Repair.

There was a lot of yelling in this case. The judge and the court attendant attempted to restore order many times. Sandra was an emotional young woman being egged on by her mother, who had not wanted to buy the boots in the first place. Billy Simpson felt his twenty-five-year reputation as a tradesman was at stake.

A critical mistake made by Sandra was her failure to bring the handbag into the store at the time she requested the dyeing of the boots. Billy's mistake was that he undertook the job

Services Performed

without having Sandra understand clearly that there was not a guarantee as to color and without clearly understanding himself the color she wanted. The judge questioned the fact that the boots were totally ruined and could not be worn again. They obviously had some value.

In the case of *Sandra Pelcher* v. *Billy Simpson's Shoe Repair,* the court awarded the sum of $30 together with the $12 amount for the dye job to be paid to Sandra Pelcher. The value of the boots was diminished to some degree, the judge believed, but there was still some value in them. Billy should have used more care in accepting the job.

Felicia Fillman's and Sandra Pelcher's cases illustrate how important it is to set out a clear agreement when dealing with artisans or tradespersons. Care should be taken by both the person who owns the product and the person who is going to perform the work. Each has an equal obligation to the other.

Checklist for Claimant

- Original sales slip.
- Receipt from artisan or tradesman.
- Copies of any documents, such as sketches, drawings, or notes given by the respondent to the claimant.
- The item that was the subject of the repair.
- Any photographs that would be helpful.
- Witnesses to agreement between the parties.

Checklist for Respondent

- Copy of any receipt.
- Copies of any documents, such as sketches, drawings, or notes given by the claimant to the respondent.
- Any physical evidence of the repair, such as a sample of product before repair to show its original condition.
- Witnesses.

Bill Haste v. Tom Stingel
CLAIM: Materials not paid for
COUNTERCLAIM: Improper painting and wallpapering services performed

Tom Stingel wanted to have the kitchen, bathroom, and living room of his house painted and wallpapered. He spent time with the decorator at Horan's, a local paint and wallpaper store, picking out wallpaper for his living room and kitchen. Tom obtained two labor estimates of $600 and then a friend told him about Bill Haste. Bill was a student who, with other college students, did painting in the summer. Tom called Bill Haste, and they agreed that for $400 Bill would paint the trim in the kitchen, living room, and bathroom, remove the existing wallpaper, and replace it with the wallpaper Tom supplied. Tom agreed to pay for the paint and various supplies Bill would need to do the work.

On the day that Bill and three of his friends arrived, Tom gave them the paint and supplies they needed. The four students immediately started stripping wallpaper, painting, and repapering. They completed the kitchen in one day. The next day, they began putting up the living-room wallpaper. Tom noticed that the color on the second roll of wallpaper was a different shade than the first. Bill Haste and his men said that was because the paper was wet as it was being put up and that it would be fine when dry.

Stingel, dissatisfied by their explanation, called an expert from Horan's: Bill McGuire, who had been in the wallpaper business for forty years, told the painters and wallpaper hangers to stop. He said it was obvious that the paper was defective and that his store would replace it.

Haste disagreed, and said that McGuire didn't know what he was talking about. He said that he, Haste, was a professional and that he would complete the job.

The second day, when all the wallpapering and painting were

completed, Haste asked for payment. Although Stingel said that he wasn't sure how the wallpaper was going to come out in the living room, he thought the painting and other wallpaper looked "okay." He paid Haste the sum of $400.

Several days later, Stingel noticed that the living-room wallpaper that McGuire had said was improperly shaded did not change as Haste had predicted. Even dry, it looked different from the other paper.

During those same several days, Haste learned that although Stingel did get $114 worth of supplies ready for Haste and his friends to use, Stingel had the supplies charged to Haste's account at the paint store. Infuriated, Haste brought this action to Small Claims Court, asking for $114 for the materials that were charged against his account. The agreement had stated that Stingel was to pay for them.

Upon being served, Stingel brought a counterclaim against Haste for $475, a figure that represented the cost of the wallpapering Haste had done in the living room (Horan's had agreed to pay for new paper); Stingel felt that he was owed $225 of this figure for repainting, because as time went on, he realized the paint job was not what he had expected. The remaining $100 was for something Stingel noticed the day after Haste left. While sitting in his kitchen drinking coffee, Stingel observed that one half of the wallpaper in his kitchen was hung upside down! Flowers that should have been growing in the normal way were hanging with stems pointed toward the ceiling.

On Stingel's and Haste's day in court, the case was called and seven people came forward. Bill Haste had brought all of his helpers, and Tom Stingel brought McGuire from the wallpaper store, and an eyewitness, the store's decorator, Miss Rainbow. Haste was very upset that Stingel had the audacity to charge the supplies to his account at the wallpaper store; and Stingel conceded that that particular claim should be awarded to Haste.

Stingel then presented his counterclaim, telling how he had

hired Haste and his men, and how they had continued to wallpaper the living room even after the expert told them to stop.

The painters then blamed the wallpaper error on the store and indicated that they should pay to have someone else take the paper down and repaper.

With regard to the upside-down paper in the kitchen, Sam Goofus, one of Haste's helpers, readily admitted that he had been confused and had hung the wallpaper upside down. He said he didn't think "it looked too bad."

As to the improper painting, the dispute centered on whether there should be one coat or two coats. Stingel said he didn't care how many coats it took, it should have looked professional.

Haste said the reason he gave him a very low estimate was that he agreed to paint just one coat. He added that he was told that the color would be the same as was currently on the walls so that one coat should have been sufficient. When he arrived, however, he found that it was a different shade that did not cover the walls completely. He said he could not do a proper job for the same price. Photographs were presented to the court substantiating the counterclaim.

Haste insisted that he did use two coats of paint on much of the job and ran out of paint twice. Three questions needed resolution by the court on the counterclaim: the upside down wallpaper, about which there was no dispute; the defective wallpaper in the living room; and the matter of additional painting.

Result: In the case of *Bill Haste* v. *Tom Stingel,* the court awarded Haste (on the original claim) the full amount of $114, plus court costs. In the counterclaim, the court awarded Stingel $200. This amount was determined by an estimate of a professional painter. It included the cost of labor to remove and replace the upside-down floral wallpaper in the kitchen ($40); the replacement cost of new wallpaper for the kitchen ($50); and the sum of $110 for the labor to remove and replace the living-room wallpaper. The claim for new painting was denied because the painter had performed the service as it had been

Services Performed

agreed. It shows that sometimes you get exactly what you pay for.

The net result was a claim in favor of the respondent against the claimant in the sum of $86. This case is an example of the use of a counterclaim. Each party had a valid claim against the other.

In presenting this type of claim on work done in your home, you can't present the improperly serviced product to the court. It is, therefore, very important that photographs be taken that clearly depict the services you claim were improperly performed.

Mabel Doyle lived in the same house for more than half a century. Over the past several years, she was having a water problem in her basement. The person she hired to plow her driveway placed the snow against her outside wall. When the snow started to melt in the spring, water seeped through the basement walls, causing it to need repainting each year. She hired Luigi Bonzai, whom she paid $250 to make the necessary repairs. Luigi promised that if he applied a special coat of bonded cement on the exterior wall, her problems would be solved. The next spring she had the same difficulty and brought a claim in Small Claims Court. Her teenage grandson had taken photographs of the work that Luigi had done. It showed that six months after the work was completed the concrete layer was cracked and had fallen off in many places. She also came to court with an estimate of repair from a mason. Luigi denied that the concrete covering had cracked until Mrs. Doyle presented the photographs in court. She was awarded her money in full.

In the services cases, you cannot just say, "It is my opinion that it was improper." The judge must have good, objective proof, just like the photographs that Mrs. Doyle presented.

CHECKLIST FOR CLAIMANT

- Original contract.
- Receipt showing payment.

- Photographs of work.
- Expert witness in court.
- Estimate to do work properly.

Checklist for Respondent

- Original contract.
- Eyewitnesses.

IMPROPER, UNNECESSARY, AND UNAUTHORIZED REPAIRS

How many times have you taken your automobile, typewriter, lawn mower, or television in for repair? You place yourself at the mercy of the person making the repair because of your lack of knowledge of the internal operations of the machine. All of us probably at some time in our lives have been taken advantage of by people having a greater mechanical skill than we. Although you should always attempt to find somebody who is reliable, this is not always possible.

After the item has been repaired, you go to pick it up and find that the bill is far in excess of what you believed it should be, or, in fact, you find that repairs were made without your authorization.

The consumer laws vary from state to state. In many areas, if a repair is going to cost more than $25, you have to give a written authorization to the repairperson. Some repairpeople also save the parts that were replaced and give them to you. In other areas, certain repair shops such as automobile garages are licensed by the state and are subject to periodic surprise inspections. Historically, women have been particularly vulnerable prey in dealing with automobile repair, as in the case of Sara Simon.

Sara Simon v. Bumper's Corner Service
CLAIM: Automobile repairs billed, but not performed

People often pay for unnecessary car repairs.

Sara Simon, a young nurse, saved her money to buy an automobile. All she could afford was an eight-year-old Buick. It looked rusted on the outside, but appeared to be in good running order, so she purchased it. The old car was quite dependable, but one day in the middle of a busy intersection, it had had enough and just quit. As Sara looked in her rear-view mirror, she happened to see a tow truck. How lucky, she thought. I can have somebody take my car out of this terrible mess and help me.

The tow-truck driver, a teenager, was happy to assist. Unable to start Sara's car, he suggested that he could tow the vehicle to his boss's service station, Bumper's Corner Service. Sara agreed. Joe Grinan, the chief mechanic, made a quick examination of the automobile. He advised Sara that the car would be ready later that afternoon and that only a minor adjustment with the carburetor would be necessary. She accepted his opinion and took a bus to work.

Later that morning, Billy Bumper, the garage owner, phoned her with bad news: It was not the carburetor, but a gear in the transmission that would have to be changed. Even though he said the cost of repair would be in excess of $400, Sara reluctantly agreed to have the repairs done because she had no other form of transportation. She was assured that the car would be ready within a few hours. Sara picked up the automobile after paying $437.52 on her charge card. The next day, the old car coughed and heaved, and once again came to a dead stop. This time Sara summoned a friend, who had a good knowledge of automobiles. He told her that it sounded like her carburetor only needed an adjustment and that he would come out and start up her car and adjust it for her, which he did free of charge.

Sara now, for the first time, sensed that Bumper's Corner Service may not have performed the proper service at all. At her friend's urging, she wanted an independent opinion. She took her once again healthy automobile to Fleet Service Center and told her story to Ken Armstrong, one of the licensed mechanics. Ken told Sara that the only adjustment Bumper's Corner Service made was to her pocketbook.

Sara Simon filed a claim against Bumper's Corner Service in Small Claims Court. First, Sara told of all of the frustration she had gone through; that she had placed her faith in Bumper's Corner Service, but it appeared that she had received either unnecessary repairs or never received any repairs at all. She documented her case with the receipts from Bumper's and a statement from the friend who repaired her vehicle. She also subpoenaed the mechanic from Fleet Service Center.

Armstrong testified that he examined the automobile and believed it was impossible that a transmission gear had been changed. He said that certain mechanical work would have had to have been done, including the changing of the valve cover gaskets. His examination showed that the gaskets were not changed, and in fact were the original dirt-covered gaskets that had probably been in the vehicle for the entire eight years of its life. Armstrong further stated that the job that Bumper's claimed that they did could not be done in an afternoon. He said the labor on the job would have taken at least sixteen hours.

Billy Bumper's only defense was, "I have the work order here. The mechanic must have done the work."

The judge inquired of Bumper, "Where is the mechanic who did the work?"

Billy said, "He's busy doing other work."

The judge wondered whether he was doing the same kind of work that he did on Miss Simon's car. Bumper, realizing that he lost his case, turned to Ken Armstrong and asked, "Does your boss know that you came over here to testify against another garage operator?"

Sara Simon had prepared her case well. It was well documented with physical evidence, and she had also subpoenaed and brought along an independent garage man to substantiate her claim. If Bumper had a valid defense, he should have brought his mechanic along to testify as to exactly what he did and to rebut anything that may have been said on behalf of Miss Simon.

Result: In the case of *Sara Simon v. Bumper's Corner Service,* the judge determined that the claimant would recover the amount in full together with interest and court costs. Another result is that Bumper's Corner Service will think twice about trying this trick on another unsuspecting person.

Ned Benson v. Country Mower Service
CLAIM: Improper lawn mower repairs

Ned Benson delivered a lawn mower that would not start to Country Mower Service for repair. Country Mower told Ned to come back in a week, at which time Ned was told the mower was working. He paid the $35.31 bill.

Ned, confident that his lawn mower would work properly, was anxious to get home to start his weekend chores. The spring rain had made the lawn thick and lush and ready for its first cutting. As soon as he arrived home, he took the mower out of the car, put gasoline in the mower, pulled the cord to start it, and . . . nothing happened.

More than a bit disappointed and frustrated, Ned went back to Country Mower Service and told the owner, Dick Petri, what had happened. Petri angrily replied, "I don't care whether it starts or not. That's your problem. I had enough trouble freeing up the lawn mower. It's just a piece of junk."

Benson picked up his equipment and headed directly to Small Claims Court to file his claim. He realized that nothing was going to be done for him by Petri or Country Mower Service.

At the time of the hearing, Ned presented his story and said simply that he paid $35.31 for repairs that were never done and he requested his money back. Dick Petri explained that this type of lawn mower was difficult to work on. He said the engine was stuck due to a lack of oil and that he added oil to free it up. He said he got it to work, replaced the starter, cleaned the carburetor, and did other work on the mower. The total amount for his services was $35.31.

Petri added that if the mower didn't work, that was Benson's problem. Petri had serviced three thousand lawnmowers, but had never seen one as bad as Benson's which, he repeated, was nothing but "a piece of junk."

Petri presented an itemized bill that indicated that the freeing up of the engine came to approximately $8.00. The other work made up the balance.

Result: In the case of *Ned Benson* v. *Country Mower Service,* the judge awarded Benson the amount of the bill less $8.00. The judge believed that Petri did try to free up the motor and may have done so. But he questioned Petri's judgment in replacing the other parts. The judge believed that Petri's experience in the business should have told him not to put any more money in this mower.

Benson relied on Country Mower's expertise and was never warned that the mower might not work once he took it home.

Christine Owens
v.
Ted Nichols d/b/a Quick Home Appliance Repair
CLAIM: Improper repair to clothes washer

Chris Owens worked long hours at her job and came home to take care of her two young sons. At the end of one summer vacation she had taken with her family, she brought home a lot of dirty laundry. It was late on Sunday night when she filled the washing machine with her children's soiled clothes. The washer filled with the right amount of water, but when it

Services Performed

came time for the rinse cycle, the water would not pump out. Frantically, she looked in her phone book for a person who might bail her out of this predicament quickly. She saw a listing for Quick Home Appliance Repair and called. Ted Nichols, who answered the phone, said he couldn't be there until first thing in the morning. Chris left the key and money for Nichols with a neighbor, because no one would be home.

When Chris came home, she found that the washer was empty, the wet clothes were in the clothes basket, and the washer was dry. On her kitchen table, she found a bill for $62.50, which had been marked "paid." The notation on the bill indicated that a new water pump had been installed at a cost of $46 and the remainder was the charge for the service call and tax. Chris was relieved that her washer was repaired, but disappointed at the high price.

After preparing her boys' dinner that evening, she put the wash in and once again, the machine filled properly with water but would not pump out. Now Chris was really angry. She tried to contact Quick Home Appliance Repair but got no answer throughout the evening.

Early the next morning, she contacted the machine manufacturer's service representative, who promised to come promptly. She left her phone number at work so that the service man could call her and tell her what the problem was. At 10:00 A.M. she received a call from the manufacturer's service representative, Mike Barry, who said that he checked the machine carefully and found a sock caught in the rubber hose leading out of the washer. This was what had caused the machine's failure to pump the water out. He removed the sock and all was fine. His bill for the service call was $18.

Chris asked about the water pump and he stated that he had checked the old pump, which was lying next to the washer, and there was nothing the matter with it.

Chris attempted to contact Ted Nichols at Quick Home Appliance Repair to tell him the story, but he never returned her calls. She then brought action in Small Claims Court against Ted Nichols d/b/a Quick Home Appliance Repair. Chris contacted the service representative, Mr. Barry, who was very glad to come into court to testify, as it was his company's policy to substantiate what has been found, if necessary, in court.

Chris Owens told the judge her story, presenting her receipt from Ted Nichols, the old pump, and the receipt from the manufacturer's service representative. Mr. Barry also told the judge what his own repair revealed. In fact, Chris Owens showed the judge the sock that was the culprit.

Ted Nichols then testified, saying that he replaced the water pump, as that is the most common cause for this type of problem. He said there was no doubt that the sock must have gotten into the machine at a later time. He stated, "This lady wanted it fixed, so I fixed it good."

Result: In the case of *Christine Owens* v. *Ted Nichols d/b/a Quick Home Appliance Repair,* judgment was rendered in full for $62.50 plus filing fees in favor of the claimant. This represented all of the bill that was paid to Nichols. Chris could not recover the amount of the manufacturer's service representative's bill because that call would have been necessary anyway.

In this case Ted Nichols left the old pump next to the washer, which made it a little easier for Chris Owens to prove her case. Anytime somebody does repairs by replacing parts, it is a good idea to insist that you retain the old parts from your equipment. This not only proves that the parts were in fact replaced, but, if you need to have another person examine them, as Chris Owens did, you will be in a better position to prove your case.

Many cases in Small Claims Court involve improper furnace repairs. As in any mechanical area in which the general public lacks knowledge, there are those who will take advantage of your ignorance. On a cold, February day when your furnace breaks down, you frantically look in the yellow pages of your phone book and call anybody to get the furnace running. If the

Services Performed

heat isn't operating, pipes could break and extensive damage could occur to your home. Worse yet, you could get really cold.

This is what happened to the Edgland family when their furnace broke down. While Byron Edgland was away at a conference late one night, his wife, Jan, felt a cold chill in their century-old home. She didn't know whom to call, but had just seen a commercial on television for Quick Heat 24-Hour Emergency Service. Twenty minutes after her call, Pluto Onsey responded. After checking the furnace for about five minutes, he told Mrs. Edgland she needed a new fan motor, two new belts, and a relay switch. The cost of the service call would be $190. She was shocked, but her choice was either to sign the authorization that evening or go without heat. She authorized the work and a half hour later Mr. Onsey was on his way with payment in full.

A week later when her husband came home, Jan told him what had happened. He immediately called over his friend Jim Elliot, who had experience in servicing furnaces while working his way through college. Jim took a quick look and immediately told Byron and Jan that the only part that had been replaced was one belt, which cost about $4.50. He pointed out to both of them the dust accumulated on the old motor, which was working fine.

Upon further inspection, it was revealed that there was no relay switch required in this furnace. The Edglands wrote a letter demanding a full refund, but were ignored. They then filed a claim in Small Claims Court.

Quick Heat was represented by its owner, Joe Quick. His only defense was that if Pluto Onsey said the work was done, it must have been done.

The judge asked Quick where the parts were. He said that as a service to the customer his serviceman always takes them out, so they don't have to bother with it.

In this case, the testimony of Jim Elliot was critical, as was the failure of Quick's repairman, Pluto Onsey, to appear in court with him. Byron and Jan Edgland were awarded the full claim.

CHECKLIST FOR CLAIMANT

- Work repair order and bill.
- Prior work repair orders to show any subsequent work done unnecessarily.
- Canceled check or charge slip.
- Any parts given to you by the repairperson.
- Statement by another repairperson after original work done (best to have expert witness present who has examined the item in question).
- Product allegedly repaired, if it is small enough to display in court.

CHECKLIST FOR RESPONDENT

- Work ticket on machine.
- Mechanic who did work should be present in court.
- Any service manual showing requirements for repair of particular defect.
- List of usual charges in area.

SERVICES RENDERED PROPERLY, BUT UNPAID

Much of the emphasis in this chapter has been on improper, unauthorized, or unnecessary services rendered. You, as the consumer, have been considered the claimant. You may also, however, be a person who performs services and does a very good job. Perhaps you were unable to obtain payment at the time the services were performed and you trusted the person whom you served, saying you would bill him or her later. You may use Small Claims Court to collect your unpaid bill.

Services Performed

It is recommended that you read all the cases in this chapter so that you can anticipate any defense that may be claimed by the people who owe you money. Be certain that you can justify your charges. The person you are suing may either say that the work was improperly done or the charge was too high and not as agreed. Sometimes there is no defense except that the respondent just doesn't have the money to pay you. In the first two instances, be prepared to justify the work you did and prove either the agreement or that the value of your services is fair in the community. This may be done either by showing standard fee schedules, such as union rates, or by producing another person in your field who can testify as to the reasonable value of services such as you performed.

If the respondent does not contest the claim, but merely states that he or she does not have the money available to pay you, you will obtain a judgment in your favor. The judge will ask the respondent what arrangements he or she can make to pay the bill. If payment is not made voluntarily, then you can follow the procedure as set out in Chapter V to collect the award.

Many professionals are not paid for their services because the public feels they have enough money and they can wait for payment. Another reason for nonpayment is that there may be a misunderstanding, as was the case with Dr. Eugene Shaw.

Dr. Eugene Shaw v. *Adolph Cuspid*
CLAIM: Unpaid professional services—dentist

Adolph Cuspid had delayed having his teeth taken care of for many, many years. His procrastination came from a combination of his fear of going to the dentist and his lack of adequate funds to pay the bill. Recently, his company's insurance plan became more comprehensive and finally included a complete dental plan. At about the same time, his teeth deteriorated to the extent that they were so painful he wanted to have them treated.

With dental plan in hand, he went to Dr. Eugene Shaw, a prominent local dentist. Dr. Shaw reviewed the dental plan and indicated that all work would be covered by the insurance provided by Cuspid's employer. He then assured Adolph that the dental work might be a bit painful, but that it was necessary if he were to have a healthy mouth. Dr. Shaw indicated that all of Cuspid's teeth would have to be removed, as most of them were totally rotten. Dr. Shaw said he would be able to remove the teeth and make a new set of teeth in a very short time.

After several visits to Dr. Shaw, Mr. Cuspid had a new set of dentures. The doctor's wife-receptionist, Phyllis, told Mr. Cuspid that he would have to sign the claim form and send it to his insurance company so that her husband could be paid for his work.

About a month later, Adolph Cuspid called Dr. Shaw's office and complained to Phyllis that his teeth didn't seem to fit right. She made an appointment for him to come in the next day for an adjustment.

Cuspid never showed up.

Dr. Shaw had completed all the work, but still had not been paid because the claim form had not been sent to the insurance company by the patient. Phyllis Shaw got no response after she urged Mr. Cuspid to send the form in. Dr. Shaw then filed a claim in Small Claims Court for the full amount of $1,000.

At the hearing, the dentist told of the patient coming to the office and the work he had done. He further stated that the reasonable value of his services was $1,000 and that he had not been paid.

The Judge then turned to Adolph to hear his side of the story, and as Cuspid started to talk, the judge was startled to see that he had no teeth. Mr. Cuspid stated that the teeth didn't fit him right and he felt uncomfortable wearing them. He then pulled them from a paper bag he was carrying and put them on the rail in front of the judge, saying, "Here, Doc, you can have them back."

Services Performed

Dr. Shaw then said, "I will be glad to make any adjustment that I have to for these teeth to fit you properly."

Upon further questioning it was learned that, although the patient did make an appointment to come in for adjustment, he never showed up. The judge then questioned Mr. Cuspid as to why he hadn't sent the insurance form in.

His response was, "I lost it."

After a little further discussion, the judge aided the parties in working out a settlement. Mr. Cuspid agreed to get a new insurance claim form, sign it, and give it to Dr. Shaw to send in. Mr. Cuspid further agreed that he would go the next day to the dentist to have the proper adjustments made.

It was obvious that in this case a minor adjustment would have benefited both parties. Dr. Shaw would receive his payment in full by the health plan covering the patient, and Mr. Cuspid would have a new set of dentures that he could wear.

Result: In the case of *Dr. Eugene Shaw* v. *Adolph Cuspid,* settled by the parties in court during the hearing.

Sometimes doctors, lawyers, dentists, or free-lance professionals such as architects and writers appear in Small Claims Court. They are not paid for their services because the work may not have been done exactly as the respondent desired In that type of case, the judge can often work out a fair resolution in court. With a minor adjustment in the work or even an explanation of the work, the respondent agrees to pay the bill in full.

There are those, however, who merely do not wish to pay for services rendered. This is often a difficult conflict to resolve, as services are not a tangible product. Once the service is performed, a person may no longer deem it a priority on bill-paying day. The use of Small Claims Court will make that bill a top priority, if the debt is valid. Professionals no longer have to be content to remain at the bottom of the pile.

Ironically, many professionals feel it is undignified to press on for their just due. However, with today's high cost of living, their attitude is changing. Show that you mean business in collecting your fees, and one short court appearance may be the only one you'll need.

Checklist for Claimant Seeking Professional Service Payment

- Contract of work to be performed.
- Records of work being performed.
- The work product or result of services, if it can be brought to court.
- Be prepared to justify your charge as usual in the area by use of brochures or fee schedules.
- Have any witnesses present who observed you performing the services.

Checklist for Respondent

- Agreement or memorandum of work to be done.
- Proof that work was improperly done by use of another witness or statement.
- Proof that fee was not as originally agreed and/or excessive (such as area fee schedule or brochure).

CHAPTER

XI

❖

Negligence

IF ANOTHER PERSON has caused you damage or harm because he or she was careless or reckless, you can bring a negligence proceeding against that person in Small Claims Court. Negligence is the failure of a person to use what is called "reasonable care," which is the care that a reasonably prudent person would exercise under similar circumstances. A negligent act is not intentional; it often appears to be an accident. For example: If a person is driving down an expressway and pulls out to pass without checking in the rear-view mirror, he may collide with your vehicle. A reasonably careful and prudent person would have looked in the rear-view mirror to see that no cars were coming. It is reasonably foreseeable that the result of the negligence or carelessness can be damage to another's automobile, specifically yours.

This, in simple terms, is the law of negligence as discussed in this chapter. It does not only apply to the highway and automobiles, as in the *Sawyer* and *Pride* cases (upcoming), but also to any nonintentional reckless or careless act. The law states universally that people have a duty not to act with negligence toward other people. The result of acting negligently is liability.

This means that the negligent person is responsible for any damages caused as the result of his act or failure to act in a prudent manner.

DEALING WITH NEGLIGENCE—
AUTOMOBILE ACCIDENT

People often refuse to accept responsibility for damage they have caused to another person or to property. Many cases heard in Small Claims Court involve motor vehicle accidents.

Do you have a negligence case that will hold up in court? The questions you must answer are:

- Was your damage the result of the other driver's careless action?
- Did he or she fail to use a standard of care that safe users of the highway would employ?
- Was that unsafe action the cause of your injury or damage?

If your answers are yes, someone is probably liable for your damage.

Most negligence cases are resolved either by your insurance company or that of the other driver without going to court. However, many accident cases do get filed in Small Claims Court. Usually there are *four* reasons for these filings:

1. The other driver notified his insurance company of the accident and gave a version of the facts that is very different from what you believe. Although you may have been offered a certain amount of the claim by the insurance company, you believe you are not at fault at all and should receive the full amount of your loss. The other driver has probably indicated that you were totally at fault. In this case it is necessary that the claim be heard by the judge.

Negligence

2. The respondent carries no insurance (even though state law requires it) and does not have the ability to pay your claim. He has, therefore, ignored any attempts to reimburse you, even though he may be at fault.

3. The other driver has insurance, but believes that you were so clearly wrong that there is no reason to notify his insurance company. He feels that if he did notify his insurance company, it would affect his rating adversely. He has chosen to defend the claim himself.

4. Your evaluation of the damage is substantially higher than that of the other party or his representative. You may, for example, believe that new parts will be required to repair your automobile, whereas the respondent may believe that used parts may be sufficient for the repair of an older vehicle. There may also be a dispute as to the replacement value of a completely demolished automobile.

If you are in an accident, the police will usually be called and will take a report. Much useful information will be contained in the report, including the name and address of the owner and driver of the other vehicle, a diagram of the accident scene, and the names of witnesses. If the other driver had liability insurance, that information is usually provided to you.

If you bring a claim, it is very important to do your homework thoroughly. You should bring a copy of the police accident report, and, if possible, ask any independent witnesses to be present in court. Be sure to talk with the witnesses in advance to find out their versions of the facts so that there will be no surprises when you get into the courtroom. As indicated before, if they will not come voluntarily, you may subpoena the witnesses.

You should also bring diagrams of the scene of the accident. These should be large enough to be seen clearly in the courtroom. Make certain that your diagrams are accurate and that an arrow indicates north. Clear photographs of the accident scene, taken from the direction of your travel at the time of the accident, would be helpful in your case. If possible, also bring photographs of the damage to each vehicle after the accident. These photos should all be clearly marked.

In proving damages, you should present two estimates from reputable repair shops. They should not merely be a total sum of repair costs, but an itemized statement of what needs to be repaired, with a breakdown of the cost for each repair. If the cost to repair your vehicle exceeds its value at the time of the accident, you will be awarded whichever is the lower amount. (See the upcoming case of *Willie Pride* v. *George Johnson*.)

The amount you can collect will vary with the law in your state. Most states now have a law of comparative negligence. This means that the judge will try to determine how much fault can be assessed to each party. If you are the claimant and if the judge believes you were 25 percent at fault, the amount of the damage you are seeking will be reduced by the sum of 25 percent. You would then receive an award equal to 75 percent of the total claim.

If you are sued, you should notify your insurance company promptly so that a representative may be present in court. If you do not do this, and an award is made against you, the company might not indemnify you in payment of the award.

This is often the case as well when the respondent files a counterclaim for damage suffered to his vehicle. You may not know of this counterclaim until the court date, as courts do not require that it be brought up in advance. If you do have liability insurance, it is important for you to ask the judge for an adjournment (a delay for another date) so that you can notify your insurance company to have a representative present. Judges usually grant this request.

If you accept a check from an insurance company before you have gone to Small Claims Court, even though you believe you are entitled to a greater amount, you may have waived your right to obtain any additional sums. In other words, you may have agreed to release the respondent from any future claim related to the accident. If you do not agree with the settlement offered and wish to pursue your claim in Small Claims Court, as did Tom Sawyer, you should not accept a partial payment from the insurance company.

Tom Sawyer v. Richard Dolan
CLAIM: Collision damage—question of liability

Thomas Sawyer was driving down Elmwood Avenue and stopped in a proper area on a two-lane road to make a left-hand turn. Along came Richard Dolan. Seeing that the car ahead of him was ready to turn left, he thought that he would go around him on the right side and continue on. When Mr. Dolan cut back into the driving lane, he took off the right fender of the Sawyer automobile, which had not yet made the left-hand turn. Both cars proceeded to the side and Dolan agreed that he had been wrong and gave all of the information, including his name, address, and insurance company to Sawyer. Sawyer then contacted Dolan's insurance company and after three weeks they wrote back to Sawyer: "We have completed our investigation and found that you were 50 percent responsible for the damage to your car. The damage was in the amount of $424. We therefore enclose a check in the amount of $212 in settlement of the claim."

Tom Sawyer was unhappy with this, so he appeared in Small Claims Court. He presented his case very thoroughly, telling what had occurred and providing his garageman's bill for the repair. The insurance company's attorney appeared and cross-examined him. In this action, even though an insurance company is involved, a claimant *must directly sue the operator of the other vehicle.* It is then the obligation of the insurance company to indemnify (reimburse) the respondent for the amount of the claim. If an award is not paid within ten days a judgment is entered in the records of the Small Claims Court that could result in a mark against the credit of the person against whom the award is made. The two parties then, instead of being claimant and respondent, become judgment creditor and judgment debtor. In this case, it was not the respondent himself who decided to defend the claim but the insurance company. It is certainly poor public relations, to say the least, for the company to permit judgment to be taken against its insured clients in cases it decided to defend.

Result: In the case of *Thomas Sawyer* v. *Richard Dolan,* the decision was made in favor of the claimant, Sawyer, in the full amount of $424 plus interest and court costs.

(In this case, the insurance company immediately forwarded the check to the court, so that no judgment would go on record against the respondent.)

Willie Pride v. *George Johnson*
CLAIM: Collision damage—question of amount entitled to

Willie Pride parked his car in a legally proper place. One evening George Johnson was driving carelessly and sideswiped the Pride automobile, causing extensive damage from the left rear tail fin to the front fender. Pride made a claim against Johnson, and at the time of the hearing, the insurance company appeared on behalf of the respondent, Johnson.

Willie Pride produced two estimates from local Cadillac dealers showing that the cost of repair would be approximately $1,950. The insurance company produced a qualified appraiser who agreed with the repair estimate but added that the automobile was a twelve-year-old Cadillac that had ninety-seven thousand miles on it. The car, therefore, had a fair market value before the accident of less than $300. To Willie, the car's worth was another matter. He indicated that this vehicle was like his child. He always took good care of it, waxed it and cleaned it and drove it down the street very proudly. He asked,

"How could this car be worth only $300 if I felt it good enough to take my family on a trip just last weekend before the accident?"

When asked by the judge how he had arrived at the $300 figure, the qualified appraiser said he had determined the price of the vehicle by checking newspaper ads and local used-car lots for comparable cars with the same mileage. He determined that the retail price of cars such as Willie's varied from $199 to $300.

Result: In the case of *Willie Pride* v. *George Johnson,* the court found in favor of Willie Pride, but only in the amount of $300. The law in most states requires that the most a person can be paid for damage to an automobile is the fair market value of the auto before the accident. In this case, if Willie's twelve-year-old Cadillac had been demolished, it would have cost thousands of dollars to rebuild. But the law does not require the car to be rebuilt if its value on the open market to the general public is less than the amount it would cost to repair the auto.

It is often difficult for someone who is harmed to accept this legal proposition. It is possible that Willie Pride could have gotten an appraiser of his own to determine that this vehicle, for some special reason, may have been worth more on the general market. For example, the tires might have been new or the engine could have been in exceptionally good condition. The car also had value as an antique. If Willie had brought with him a professional appraiser who had inspected the automobile either before or after the accident, it would have strengthened his claim and he would have received a greater award. But without expert testimony, the court had to rely on the figures submitted by a reliable and qualified appraiser of automobiles. This does not mean that the judge has to accept fully what the appraiser says. The judge may question the appraiser and modify the amount to some small extent.

Checklist for Claimant

- Accident report.
- Two estimates of repair of damage.
- Photographs of automobile and accident scene.
- Sketch or diagram of area where accident happened.
- If damage exceeds fair market value of car, a qualified appraiser can provide documentation of unusual merits, such as antique value.

Checklist for Respondent

- Notify your insurance company.
- Accident report.
- Your own estimate of claimant's damage.
- Photographs of automobile and accident scene.
- Sketch or diagram of area where accident happened.
- If damage exceeds fair market value of car, an expert appraiser can provide documentation of current value.

NEGLIGENCE BY WORKMEN

Todd Riley v. *SPL Contractors, Inc.*
CLAIM: Damage to automobile from paint overspray

Todd Riley had just purchased a brand new sportscar with special sparkling metallic paint, striping, and three-tone deluxe exterior. He had waited three months for the car to arrive.

Todd worked at the local brewery, whose manufacturing plant was located on a riverbank. The employee parking lot was adjacent to the river, and part of the parking was almost underneath High View Bridge. For several weeks, Todd parked his car in the lot when he arrived at work, and inspected the car daily to see that it was in good condition. Each evening, when he got home, he would wash and polish it.

One day in July he came out of work and found particles of red all over the car's hood, front fenders, windshield, and top. He became very excited and upset, but recalled that contractors had begun painting High View Bridge that day. Although the car was parked some three-hundred feet away, it was certainly downwind of the bridge. Todd learned that friends of his found their cars with these red flecks on them, so they got together and contacted the manager of their company, who said that the state bridge authority had hired SPL Contractors, Inc., to paint the bridge.

The following day, the brewery personnel director told Todd that SPL would be contacting him to repair any damage they had caused to his car. A clause in the SPL contract called for taking all necessary precautions to avoid such an overspray. A specific clause in the contract prohibited any painting if the wind exceeded 10 mph. On that day, wind gusts had been recorded up to 25 mph, yet painting had continued.

Several days later, a representative from SPL, Mr. Dudley Wright, appeared at the parking lot and offered Todd some solvent and a rag to attempt to remove the paint spray from the car. Todd refused to do the work himself. He feared that he would damage the car's exterior and preferred that a professional remove the paint.

The SPL representative, himself, began to remove the red flecks from the windshield. As he did so, the windshield became scratched and clouded. Further conversation between Todd and Mr. Wright from SPL resulted in the latter's offer to have one of SPL's representatives completely clean the car.

Todd, being very proud of his new automobile, which represented a substantial investment, decided he would prefer to take the car back to the dealer for repair. After he discussed the matter fully with the dealer's representative, it was concluded that Todd's car would need a new windshield and professional repainting of the car. Cost of the whole job was set at $861. When the estimate was presented to SPL Contractors, Mr.

Wright refused to consider it. He added that now nothing would be paid since Todd shouldn't have parked his car near the bridge in the first place.

Todd Riley decided his remedy was Small Claims Court. He appeared with three of his friends and methodically addressed each issue. First he told the judge that he had always parked his car in the same spot and was never warned about the bridge painting. He presented a report from the United States Weather Bureau showing that the wind had reached 25 mph on the day in question. The bill of sale showed the cost of the new car and the fact that it was just a few weeks old at the time of the damage. He then presented pictures of the actual damage and a closeup of the red flecks of paint. To all of this, he added his story of Mr. Wright's attempt to remove the paint with some solvent and the subsequent damage to the windshield. He also presented a certified estimate from the dealership where he bought the car, stating what it would cost to put the car back in new condition. Finally, he had his witnesses tell of his reaction when he found the paint on the vehicle.

The judge was anxious to hear the defense presented by Dudley Wright, of SPL Contractors, Inc. In court he admitted that his company caused the spray, but stated that the car should not have been parked there. He further stated that as soon as he found out about the damage, he attempted to remove the overspray from the car himself; or give Riley enough solvent to do it; or have one of his painters work on the car.

The judge asked if any warning was given to the people in the brewery about the painting to be done.

Dudley Wright's answer was, "No, there was no warning, but they certainly could have seen our equipment up there." He added, "Judge, if you do find that we are negligent in this matter, we shouldn't have to pay the bill in full because we said that we would take care of it in our own way."

Result: In the case of *Todd Riley* v. *SPL Contractors, Inc.,* the judge ruled for the claimant in the full amount of $861. In this case, the respondent had an obligation to warn anybody who could sustain damage by parking near the bridge. Riley had parked there on a regular basis with other workers. He assumed he could safely park his new automobile in the same place it had been for several weeks.

The company was also found negligent for painting on a windy day with the knowledge it could be damaging to people's property (and perhaps to people's health as well). In awarding the full amount, the judge believed that Todd Riley had a right to have his car restored to its original condition. He felt Riley should not have to repair the damage himself or permit a possibly unskilled person to work on the car.

The claimant in this case documented his claim in a methodical and thorough manner. As a further result of the decision, SPL paid all other outstanding claims to the other people who suffered damage.

Todd Riley was able to obtain a copy of the contract between the state bridge authority and SPL Contractors through the influence of his employer. If you are in a similar situation, you can compel a person in possession of a contract to produce it in court. Ask the clerk to issue a *subpoena duces tecum* and direct it to the person who is holding the relevant contract. (See "Your Meeting with the Clerk" in Chapter III.) You can obtain any written record that is important in the presentation or defense of a claim through this procedure. The *subpoena duces tecum* is in effect an order of the court requiring a person or corporation to produce documents that are *relevant* to your case. The clerk will tell you that you must make a specific request and not a general request for a mass of documents that are not on the point. Any reports from a municipality or city regarding the incident can be obtained by the same procedure if you cannot get them voluntarily.

Cases similar to Todd Riley's have occurred when bricks falling from buildings, and objects falling out of windows injure persons or property.

In the case of falling bricks, you can be successful in court if you can prove that the owner of the building knew or should have known of the dangerous conditions, and that the damage caused was reasonably foreseeable. This is sometimes hard to prove; however, you can, through your investigation, follow the same procedure that Todd Riley did.

Have you ever been in traffic behind a truck when debris has blown off of it, striking your windshield and breaking it? In this case, you can make a prompt report of the accident to the police and you should have no trouble recovering from the operator of the truck. If the claim is denied or if there is a question as to the amount, your option in Small Claims Court is still available.

CHECKLIST FOR CLAIMANT IN AUTO DAMAGE— OVERSPRAY

- Bill of sale or title certificate to new automobile.
- Photographs of automobile before (if possible) and after damage.
- Any other documents showing negligence; in this case, United States Weather Bureau charts (easily obtainable at local weather bureau for nominal sum).
- Estimate of repair from reputable dealer of your choice.
- Any witnesses to support your claim.
- Copy of contractor's agreement with relevant clause highlighted, local ordinances relating to environmental pollution and/or community health hazards, etc.

CHECKLIST FOR RESPONDENT

- Proof you were not using the color paint as claimed.
- Statement you were not working on the day claimed.
- Reputable dealer's estimate that may be different from claimant's

NEGLIGENCE WHILE PERFORMING SERVICE

John Mooney
v.
Sam White d/b/a Bright and Shine Car Wash

CLAIM: Damage in car wash

John Mooney owned a small American car, which he decided to run through a car wash he had never used before. Sam White's Bright and Shine Car Wash was a completely automated wash; the driver stayed inside the car while a chain pulled the vehicle through. As the car moved along, it passed guidesticks, which activated the different cleaning processes—one stick started the soap spray, another the brushes, until the car finally entered the wind tunnel for drying.

As John prepared to enter the car wash, he was told by the car-wash operator to keep his hands off the steering wheel and to leave the engine running with the car in neutral. He obliged, paid his $2.00, and drove up to the entrance. Although he was unfamiliar with this particular car wash, he thought he heard a brief screeching noise while the brushes were operating. At the end of the wash, he got out of the car to do some additional drying. He noticed two new scratches on the right side of his car, one of which was deep. He contacted the manager and owner of the wash, Sam White.

Sam came over and looked at the damage and said that it did not happen in his wash. John Mooney refused to move his car unless White admitted liability. White believed that this type of scratch had to be caused in some other way. As the next three cars pulled out of the wash, Mooney, White, and the driver of each car inspected the vehicles and saw no damage to them. They then walked the line and went back to look at the machine, but they found nothing that could have caused the damage. The brushes were soft, there was no defect in the machine, and no evidence of chrome strips that might have been caught up in the machine.

Mooney still insisted that the damage was caused by the car wash and told White he would see him in Small Claims Court.

In preparation of his claim, John Mooney took photographs showing the damage to his automobile. He also went to a collision shop and obtained a statement of damage in the amount of $55.26 and a statement indicating that the damage was fresh on the day he brought it in, the same day as the incident.

Both Mooney and White appeared in Small Claims Court. Mooney related his side of the story, saying that he saw the scratches after getting out of the car, and remembered hearing an unusual sound from the right side of the car during the car wash.

Sam White stated that there was no way that the scratches could have been caused by his car wash and that both he and Mooney had looked at three vehicles coming out of the wash after Mooney's and further inspected the equipment.

The court then inquired as to whether the guide bars that activate the machines could have been defective and scratched the car in some way. The owner of the wash agreed that the bars were sharp, but noted that they were wrapped with rubber. He said he had inspected them and they appeared to be fine on the day of the incident. These bars are also on the left side of the car, and the damage in this case was only on the right side.

Result: In the case of *John Mooney* v. *Sam White d/b/a Bright and Shine Car Wash,* the judge ruled no cause for action. The court felt that John Mooney sincerely believed that the car wash caused his damage. However, there was a lack of proof other than some circumstantial evidence that the car wash caused the damage. Sam White denied that it could have happened in his wash. He proved that point directly after the incident by showing Mooney three additional cars that went through unscathed, and by inspecting the wash.

Although Mooney did bring in an estimate with the opinion

Negligence

that the damage was fresh, the judge felt it could have occurred earlier that day.

During this trial, the judge did try to arrive at a compromise by asking Sam White to pay some of the claim out of good will. He refused, noting that this was the first time this person used his car wash.

"I don't know why I owe any good will to him," he said, "especially when he accused my car wash of doing something that it just didn't do."

CHECKLIST FOR CLAIMANT

- Receipt showing payment for wash if one was given.
- Any police report made at the time.
- Estimate to repair damage.
- Any physical evidence such as a broken chrome strip that may have fallen off or a broken mirror.
- Clear photographs of car before (if possible) and after damage.

CHECKLIST FOR RESPONDENT

- Person who operated the car wash at the time of the incident.
- Proof that no other vehicles were damaged that day.
- Proof that the manager at the time in question had inspected the wash line.

DAMAGE TO YOUR GOODS BY NEGLIGENCE WHILE IN POSSESSION AND CONTROL OF OTHERS

Just think how many times during the course of a year you entrust something you own to another person. You may be loaning the item for the other person's benefit, such as loaning your automobile, an item of clothing, or even a book to a friend. Or the transaction could be for your benefit only, such as when a person lets you store an item without charge in his custody.

The most common entrusting is for mutual benefit. This includes something as simple as checking your coat in a restaurant. In that situation, a person takes your coat, hangs it on a hook, and you give them some money as a checking charge. While the coat is in the possession of the other person, he or she is holding it in a position of trust for you. These examples are called "bailments" in the law.

In each situation if damage occurs to the item you have placed in trust, there is a presumption that the person who held the item was negligent. The other person can overcome that presumption, indicating he or she was not at fault in the loss or destruction of the item, by stating how he or she exercised care over the product. The two cases that follow are common in Small Claims Court. Both Harriet Tiffany and Carol Satinaw entrusted their personal items to others.

Harriet Tiffany v. Bright Dry Cleaners, Inc.
CLAIM: Improper dry-cleaning services—damage to fabric

Now that the Tiffany children were at an age at which they would no longer jump on the couch and spill food on the carpet, Harriet and Richard Tiffany decided to redecorate their home. They hired an interior decorator and ordered a new couch and love seat in a soft yellow and green textured fabric. The furniture arrived and was exactly as Harriet Tiffany had pictured it. She selected carpet to match the color of the furniture. Harriet and her decorator then carefully chose wall coverings and draperies to complement the new color scheme.

Although Harriet was a meticulous housekeeper, the family did use the room often, and the furniture became soiled. After a year passed, she decided to freshen the fabric on the couch

Negligence

and love seat by removing the cushion covers and taking them to Bright Dry Cleaners to be cleaned. Harriet removed eighteen cushion covers from the two pieces of furniture and took them all at one time.

When Harriet delivered the covers to the dry cleaners, the clerk told her there would be no problem, but it would be about two weeks before the job could be completed. Harriet was annoyed with the time delay because she could not use her living room during that time, but she agreed to have the covers drycleaned.

Two weeks later, she picked up the covers and paid the sum of $30.90 for the cleaning. When she got them home, she examined the fabric and was shocked! The material had changed color. The yellow had turned green and the original green had lightened. She immediately contacted John Davis, the manager of Bright Dry Cleaners. He asked her to bring the covers back, which she did, and he said he would try to clean them again in an attempt to change the color back. After cleaning two of the covers, it was obvious to John that he was only making the situation worse. He said he was sorry, but there was nothing that could be done. Mrs. Tiffany would just have to live with the situation.

Mrs. Tiffany brought an action in Small Claims Court. She came to court with all of the covers from her couch, including one pillow, which she had forgotten to take to the dry cleaners. She then told her story, indicating that when she went to the dry cleaners, the clerk neither warned her that the work might not be done properly nor asked her to sign a release of any liability. There were no signs in the premises indicating that the cleaner would not be responsible for any damage to the fabric. She presumed that the respondent was an expert, and that if the material were accepted for cleaning, it would be done properly.

Mrs. Tiffany showed the judge the striking difference in the fabric color before and after the cleaning. It was apparent that the color scheme was totally the reverse of the original. Mrs. Tiffany sued for a complete replacement of both the love seat and the couch for a total of $928.

John Davis, on behalf of Bright Dry Cleaners, indicated that he had had the fabric examined by a special laboratory to determine why the cushion covers lost and changed color. The lab report, which he presented, indicated that the fabric originally contained material that was soluble in dry-cleaning solvent. The report further stated that the problem was not caused by mishandling in dry cleaning. His position was that Bright Dry Cleaners did nothing wrong.

Harriet Tiffany then stated that she knew nothing about fabric and relied totally on the expertise of the professional dry cleaner. She believed they shouldn't have agreed to clean the fabric, or that they should at least have warned her that there might be a problem in dry cleaning. The judge then asked John Davis if any warning had been given to Mrs. Tiffany.

Davis sheepishly said, "No, we had a new clerk on duty, and there was no warning given. We normally have a release signed, but the girl who took in the material made a mistake." He added that it was the fault of the manufacturer of the fabric for not warning Mrs. Tiffany, not that of the dry cleaner.

The judge then asked Harriet Tiffany if she had found out how much it would cost to reupholster the cushions with either the same material or to reupholster the couch and love seat with new fabric. She presented an estimate that far exceeded the original purchase price of the couch. The judge then asked her what the salvage value would be to sell the couch and love seat to another buyer who did not care that the colors were not the same. She said that she had obtained an estimate from a used-furniture dealer of $400.

Result: In the case of *Harriet Tiffany* v. *Bright Dry Cleaners, Inc.,* the decision was in favor of the claimant in the amount of

$527, which represents the difference between the purchase price of the furniture and the salvage value, together with the additional amount of $30.90 for the dry-cleaning bill, and court costs.

The claimant, Harriet Tiffany, had done her homework well. Not only had she brought into court demonstrative evidence (the actual goods damaged), but she also brought in the sales slip showing that there was no disclaimer or warning by the dry cleaner. She had determined what the original cost of the product was and its salvage value.

Mrs. Tiffany had relied upon the expertise of Bright Dry Cleaners. Once they accepted the fabric without warning the customer, they also accepted liability for any damage to it. Although the dry cleaner may be free of any negligence in acting improperly in the cleaning process, they were negligent in not warning the customer of a possible problem. They were also negligent in going ahead with the job when a risk was evident.

In this case, if the dry cleaner had explained to Mrs. Tiffany the risks involved and actually had her sign a disclaimer or release, there would have been no liability to them. She would have accepted the risk.

In another case, Phyllis Morrison had recently purchased a multicolored rabbit fur coat. She wanted to keep it safe for the summer and took it for storage to No Spots Dry Cleaning and Storage. She received a temporary receipt and was told that within about two weeks she would receive her full contract and permanent receipt. As time went by, she received no additional paperwork.

About a year later she took her temporary receipt to the branch store of the No Spots Dry Cleaning and Storage and was told that it would take a few days to locate her coat. Several days went by and she contacted Dick Wiles, the manager. He acknowledged that Mrs. Morrison had a valid receipt, but was unable to find the coat or any additional paperwork. His only defense was that if he didn't have the coat, Mrs. Morrison must have had somebody pick it up for her. Under oath, she testified that "Nobody picked anything up," and that the value of the coat was $500. She presented a receipt showing the purchase price, and an estimate of replacement for the same amount. Mr. Wiles said he was sorry, but he could not understand what happened to the coat.

The judge's decision, based upon the receipt and the sworn testimony of Mrs. Morrison, was to award the full value to her. At the hearing, Mr. Wiles acknowledged that a clerk who no longer worked at that outlet may never have turned the coat in to the main company for storage.

There is absolute liability for lost goods as long as the owner of the clothing keeps the receipt, and the dry cleaner can show no proof of returning it to the owner.

Checklist for Claimant in Damaged or Lost Goods Case

- Original bill of sale showing price of product when purchased.
- Goods that were damaged or lost.
- Any slips or receipts given at the time the defendant accepted the product for service.
- Estimate of replacement value or proper repair.
- Estimate of salvage value of goods damaged.
- Any professional manuals or reports regarding handling of goods.

Checklist for Respondent

- Any disclaimer or document signed by the customer showing a release of liability.
- Any receipt or sales slip of the transaction.
- Any professional report showing cause of damage.
- Estimate of replacement or repair of customer's goods.

Carol Satinaw v. We Park 'em, Inc.
CLAIM: Auto damage in parking lot

Miss Satinaw drove into the city for her annual dentist appointment. She circled the block a few times until she found a parking lot that appeared to have some empty spaces. Usually, she left her car at a lot where she could park and lock the car herself, but on this day the only space available was in a lot run by We Park 'em, Inc.

Although she was not too happy about the idea of somebody else driving her car, which had just been freshly painted, Miss Satinaw had no choice. As she drove in, she was greeted by a teenage boy who was one of two parking attendants. He asked her how long she would be, and she told him, "About an hour." He then gave her a ticket, told her that he would park the car, and that she could reclaim her car with the ticket. He jumped into the car and drove it to the back of the lot.

After her dental checkup was completed, Miss Satinaw returned to the parking lot, ticket and money in hand. The teenage attendant was gone and an older man asked her what kind of car she had. She described her car and he asked her to look around for it, as he was not sure where the boy had parked it.

She walked around for about ten minutes before she found her car and said she could drive it out herself. As she approached the door on the driver's side, she noticed a new dent and scratch nearly two feet long starting at the passenger door and going toward the rear. She immediately summoned the older gentleman, whom she later found to be the manager. He said he didn't know how that could have happened in his lot.

Miss Satinaw then checked the car next to her. Although she found no dents, she found scrapings of green paint, the same color as her automobile, on the bumper. She pointed this out to the manager, who told her to get a repair estimate. He would, in the meanwhile, interrogate the young man who was parking cars.

Miss Satinaw was not pleased about the situation, but she did go to a couple of garages and obtained two estimates, one for $136 and another from the dealer who had just painted the car, for $148. When she sent these to the corporate offices of We Park 'em, Inc., she was told that the damage could not have occurred in the parking lot. She then filed her claim in Small Claims Court.

At the time she met with the clerk, Miss Satinaw gave her the names of the parking lot manager and the young attendant who had parked her car. She had them both subpoenaed to appear in court.

On the day of the hearing, Miss Satinaw appeared with photographs of the damaged car, the two estimates, and the work order for the repairs and painting, which had just been completed a few days before the incident.

We Park 'em, Inc., was represented by an attorney, as was required, because We Park 'em was a publicly-held corporation, and the manager from the parking lot, Gary Brinty, appeared. Miss Satinaw told the court that she just had her car repainted a special British racing green and she recounted how she had found the same paint on the front bumper of the car parked next to hers.

Mr. Brinty said that he had observed the same thing. He said, however, he had not been able to find the young man who had parked the car because the teenager never came back to pick up his paycheck. The corporate attorney stated that because the young man had not been found, the investigation was not yet completed by We Park 'em, Inc. Therefore they were unable to pay the claim.

Billy Denton, the young man, never returned to the lot. He was not even available to have the subpoena served on him.

Result: In the case of *Carol Satinaw* v. *We Park 'em, Inc.,* an award was granted in favor of the claimant in the full amount of $148. This represented the amount of the estimate from the dealer who had just painted the automobile. Inasmuch as the claimant had already had work done by this garage, it made sense for the repair to be done at the same place.

Although no one actually saw Billy Denton cause the damage to the car, in this case circumstantial evidence pointed to his negligence. Miss Satinaw promptly looked around to see if she could find damage on other automobiles. Not only did she find it, but she also pointed it out to the manager so that he could not deny it at the time of the hearing.

In this case, the parking-lot owner assumed complete responsibility for the vehicle when he or his agent (Billy Denton) was given the key. If the damage had not been fresh and Miss Satinaw was unable to locate paint on another vehicle in the lot, she would have had difficulty proving her case. It would have come down to a question of fact between the claimant and the representative of We Park 'em, Inc.

Many times parking-lot attendants are blamed for damage that is not done while the vehicle is under their care. It is a good idea always to check your car before you leave it in the hands of a parking-lot attendant and inspect it carefully before driving away. If you have anyone with you, he or she should witness both inspections. If you do discover damage, it is very important to file a report immediately. A timely report is helpful for a judge who is considering the merits of the claimant's case.

In parking lots in which the owner of the car parks and locks the car himself, one is merely renting space. The owner of this type of lot is not liable for any damage to your car. It is the same as parking in the street.

CHECKLIST FOR CLAIMANT

- Photograph of damage.
- Estimate of repair.
- Subpoena any employees of the respondent who may be helpful to your case.
- Make copies of any reports showing the complaint.

- If work had just been done to your car, bring copies of bill.
- Bring any witnesses of the incident to court.

Checklist for Respondent

- Photograph of damage.
- Estimate of repair.
- Employee charged with care of item.

CHAPTER

XII

Heartbreak Cases

HAVE YOU EVER been involved in a loving relationship of trust and caring that suddenly disintegrated? All of the closeness you shared is gone. While things were going well you probably shared items of personal property, things that represented your promises and plans for a future together. Now that your relationship has soured, you have to determine who has the right to the property, a decision that is complicated by the anger and hurt feelings that often accompany the end of loving relationships.

Heartbreak cases involve roommates, friends, and lovers, as well as people who were living together as husband and wife but were never formally married. They also involve those who had plans to get married at a future date, but broke the engagement, and others whose relationships were built on feelings and emotions rather than business.

As the relationship changes from one of harmony to one of disruption, many problems arise involving payment of money, ownership of personal property, and responsibility for certain bills that were incurred by each partner while together. All these matters are subject to litigation in Small Claims Court.

Often this type of case comes into court disguised as a simple dispute between strangers, but the judge is quickly able to sense that a closer relationship once existed between the parties. Judges feel that it is not only important for people to use the court to settle disputes and set monetary damages, but that the court is also useful in helping the parties express their feelings toward one another. In many hearbreak cases, communication has broken down. The only way the relationship can be finally resolved is through an airing of differences before the Small Claims Court judge.

Heartbreak cases often become very difficult. The drama in court unfolds, the people are tense, and the issue of who owes what may be merely a way to air hurt and hostility. In these cases, Small Claims Court is therapeutic. The award may not be as important as the opportunity the court has given people to have the last word.

Luella Greenly v. *Gus Lombard*
CLAIM: Personal property not returned

Four years before, Luella Greenly was a hardworking widow with four small boys, just approaching their teenage years. She met Gus Lombard at a Church gathering, and they became fast friends. Mrs. Greenly was about to be put out of her apartment for her inability to pay the rent and feed her children at the same time, when Mr. Lombard told her that he had an empty house and would sure like to have Mrs. Greenly and her four boys move in. He had always longed for a family.

Although Mrs. Greenly and Lombard did not marry, she and her boys all lived together with Lombard as a family during the next three years. Lombard provided shelter and Mrs. Greenly provided housekeeping chores and food money. She also brought several items into the home, including small kitchen appliances, some curtains, tools, Christmas decorations, and cooking utensils. During these years, Lombard purchased many items that he gave as gifts to Mrs. Greenly and her family, including a camera and other small appliances. As Mrs. Greenly and her boys had had a difficult life before meeting Lombard, this semblance of a family gave them a feeling of security. The arrangement was fine, except there was no marriage.

Abruptly, just after their third Christmas together, Lombard told the family to leave. He said it was his house, they had been his tenants, and they should not come back. They refused to go. Lombard, with help from a friend, moved to the curb in front of the house all of the personal items he felt Mrs. Greenly should have and locked the door.

Mrs. Greenly, believing she had been cheated out of property that belonged to her, brought an action in Small Claims Court for $1,000, the maximum claim in that local court. She asked for compensation for the sewing machine, the camera, Christmas decorations, and other household items. She also wanted $120, money she said Lombard took from the children, who had earned it doing jobs in the neighborhood.

At the time of the hearing, Mrs. Greenly appeared with her four children, who were now a bit older. They all had shabby clothes but bright faces as they explained their mother's plight.

Lombard was outnumbered, but he spoke up. He stated that the Greenly family were only tenants in his house, that he provided shelter and heat and paid all the utilities for this family and got nothing but aggravation in return. He said that he never intended a personal relationship to develop and that he should have charged rent. He told the judge that the sewing machine, floor-to-ceiling draperies, and other household items were all items he purchased for the house and not for the people in it. He further said that taking the money from the boys was justified in that the money defrayed household expenses that he incurred on their behalf. Lombard said he felt justified in putting all of the items that the Greenlys brought into the house at the curb. If Mrs. Greenly failed to claim them, the refuse collector would. When asked if there was any other item that was taken by Lombard, Mrs. Greenly said, "Yes, he took the ring back too."

It was obvious to the judge that this action involved a great deal of emotion and disappointment between the parties because of the termination of their relationship. The judge permitted the parties to express their feelings toward one another as a final means of communication, then looked beyond the emotion the parties had experienced, and rendered a decision based on the facts.

Result: In the case of *Luella Greenly* v. *Gus Lombard,* judgment was made in favor of the claimant in the amount of $350, which represented items that belonged to her prior to the living arrangement and which were not returned, less the depreciation of their value; and $120 representing cash belonging to two of the children. The total award was $470, plus the filing fee.

In this type of case, the sadness comes through. As is often the case, the relationship between the adults deeply affects the children. Their hopes of having a father again were dashed and replaced by anger. The experience in court gave all of the children an opportunity to be heard, to tell a person in authority their side of the story.

The judge wrote a decision urging all parties to put the past behind them and look toward building a future without one another. He told them that dwelling in the past could only result in additional pain to all.

CHECKLIST FOR CLAIMANT

- List of items claimed by claimant and family.
- Purchase price or replacement value with proof, either advertisements or price list.
- Any photographs of personal items not returned.
- Any documents or witnesses to prove relationship between parties.

CHECKLIST FOR RESPONDENT

- Canceled checks for any payments made on behalf of claimant or family.
- Any photographs to prove case.
- Any witnesses to indicate what conversations had taken place between the parties.

Kevin Brown v. Eileen Sander
CLAIM: Return cost of one half of furniture

Kevin and Eileen were young people who had dreams of a bright future together. They had been friends throughout their high-school years. As they entered their twenties, they became engaged to be married soon. Kevin purchased an $800 ring for Eileen. Soon after, they went out together looking for furniture for the apartment they would share after their marriage. They spent $1,200 on a new bedroom set, which they temporarily stored at Eileen's parents' home. Kevin and Eileen had each contributed one half of the cost of the set.

As the wedding date approached, they held many long discussions and decided together that they would not be happy as husband and wife. Both were sad, but neither was at fault. The decision they made was rational and intelligent, but not without pain. Eileen gave Kevin the ring back.

Several days later, Kevin attempted to discuss the issue of the bedroom set. Eileen (on the advice of her mother) said she felt that by returning the ring, she could keep the bedroom set. Kevin felt that he was entitled to the sum of $600, or his contribution for the furniture, and brought action against Eileen for that sum.

At the time the case was called, Kevin, Eileen, and her mother came forward. Kevin and Eileen related the facts without dispute. Then Eileen's mother took over. She told the judge that her daughter had given back a perfectly beautiful ring, which should be enough to satisfy Kevin. The breakup, she said, was not Eileen's fault, but Kevin's because he was more interested in playing basketball with the boys than in spending time with Eileen. It appeared to the judge as if she were the one advising her daughter and the one who was most let down that Kevin and Eileen would not be walking to the altar together. Both of the young people seemed embarrassed. The judge felt that they wanted to do the fair thing. Eileen's mother appeared to be the instigator of this lawsuit.

Result: In the case of *Kevin Brown* v. *Eileen Sander,* the judge awarded the claimant $600 plus the costs of the action. In his ruling, the judge felt that the young people should be returned, as nearly as possible, to the way they were before the ring was purchased. He therefore ordered that Kevin retain the ring, and Eileen retain the furniture (if she wished) after reimbursing Kevin for his contribution.

The judge silently hoped Eileen would move out of her mother's house, so Eileen could make her own decisions.

Millie Hagger v. *William Short*
CLAIM: Money due and owing based on promise to pay

Miss Hagger brought this action for $88.62, requesting reimbursement for monies she said she loaned Mr. Short. Miss Hagger and Mr. Short had been living together for six months and had great hopes for the future of their relationship. This relationship apparently had ended; the judge noticed that Miss Hagger brought another man to court with her for moral support. She testified that when she and Mr. Short were friends, he had suggested that they have their picture taken together and order two 8 x 11s and several wallet-size prints.

When it came time to pay at the photographic studio, Mr. Short had no money so he asked Miss Hagger to pay for the photographs. She put it on her charge card and off they went

Heartbreak Cases

with the photographs.

Sometime later, Bill Long came into the relationship, by moving into the spare bedroom. Although Miss Hagger insisted that Mr. Long merely moved in as a tenant, William Short disagreed and said that he smartened up and moved out.

In Court, Miss Hagger said that she would be willing to give Mr. Short the photograph of the two of them (holding hands), if he would pay her the money as he said he would. Mr. Short stood silent in the courtroom, apparently hurt and bewildered. Long stared at Short, who seemed afraid to say anything. The judge, sensing Short's fear, asked the court attendant to step forward. He then ordered Long to have a seat and asked Short to speak.

Mr. Short began slowly to tell a long story about how he and Miss Hagger had lived together for several months and how Millie Hagger had never worked a day. He said he turned over all of his payroll checks to her and that she was the one who wanted to have the photographs taken so that she could send them to friends in Wyoming. He said he never agreed to pay for the photographs and that she was merely trying to collect money that was not due to her. He further said that three days after they obtained the photographs, Millie Hagger brought Bill Long into the house and all three lived together until Short decided not to put up with it any longer. He stated that as he was cleaning out dresser drawers, in preparation for moving out, he found four more photographs of Millie and other men in the same smiling pose.

Millie's only retort was, "If he'll settle for half right now in court, he can have the picture." The judge interrupted the proceeding and told the parties it would be best for them not to have any further contact with one another. They would receive the decision in the mail.

Result: In the case of *Millie Hagger* v. *William Short,* the Judge ruled no cause for action. The judge reserved decision to avoid a fist fight in Court between the new and the used, the

Long and the Short. The judge hoped that Miss Hagger's pattern would not continue to hurt other people in the future, and that maybe Bill Long would see this court experience as revealing of his future.

Cases involving heartbreak occur on a regular basis. A college professor who had fallen in love with one of his students had sent for her to visit with him on a summer sabbatical in Spain. After they spent several days together, a falling out occurred and the young lady was left overseas without money and without a return ticket home. She did finally wire for money and was able to obtain a return passage to the States. When she arrived back, she started an action for breach of agreement against her former boyfriend on the basis of misrepresentation and failure to provide a return trip home.

It was a most difficult case, as the entire relationship was aired in Small Claims Court. Finally the parties worked out a settlement whereby the professor exchanged an art object he owned for the cost of her return trip. It was a unique settlement for an unusual case.

Other cases deal with division of responsibility for rents that were due when one of the friends left the property without paying his or her share. Many other cases involve responsibility for long-distance telephone calls.

Heartbreak cases can be cross-referenced with the sections on promissory notes and contracts in Chapter VI, as well as the areas of intentional damage and missing goods in Chapter XV. You also will find some common factors among the other case areas.

Checklist for Both Claimant and Respondent

- Receipts for items purchased.
- Witnesses to any agreement between the parties.
- Canceled checks or other documents.

CHAPTER

XIII

Claims in which a Child Is a Party

IN SMALL CLAIMS COURT, children are people too!

A person is considered a child or an infant (the legal term for a child) by the law if he or she has not reached the age of majority, the age at which a person is legally responsible for his or her own actions and debts. The age differs from state to state, from eighteen to twenty-one years old.

Rules in many localities prohibit a claim from being brought in the name of the infant alone. In these states, an infant may bring a claim to Small Claims Court by naming a guardian, who is usually the parent of the young person.

Some states require an application for permission to proceed. This is provided by the clerk of Small Claims Court. In most states, however, the parent need only go to the clerk's office with the child to sign a claim form. The parent may commence the action as "John Jones, parent of Pamela Jones, an infant."

If the young person is over the age of fourteen, even though not yet of the age of majority, he or she will be asked to sign the claim form also. It is a simple procedure not unlike an adult filing a claim on his or her own behalf.

This procedure does not preclude the young person from

telling the whole story in court. There are rules, however, regarding the administration of an oath to someone under the age of eleven. If a person younger than eleven must testify, the child can tell the judge what occurred, but it is not considered with the same weight as the testimony of someone who understands the nature of an oath (a promise to tell the truth).

The parent or guardian should also appear in Small Claims Court with the young person at the time of the hearing. That's what Kathy Williams did on behalf of her son, Tommy, in their case against Ethel Caine.

ACTIONS BY INFANTS

Kathy Williams, as Parent of Tommy Williams
v.
Ethel Caine

CLAIM: Replace clothing damaged from dog bite

Tommy Williams was eleven years old and earned money doing odd jobs in his neighborhood. He cut lawns, washed windows, and shoveled snowy sidewalks. Often, on the way to his job, Tommy had to walk by a house owned by Ethel Caine, who was not the friendliest of neighbors. She owned a bulldog named Sparky, which Tommy thought looked ferocious. All the kids in the neighborhood gave Sparky wide berth and avoided going anywhere near Mrs. Caine's house. Mrs. Caine often left the dog tied to a long leash outside the house and he often paced the length of the leash, glaring at all who passed.

Mrs. Caine asked Tommy to do some work around her house, raking leaves and cleaning up the yard. When the snow fell, she asked Tommy to keep her front sidewalk clear. Although Tommy was frightened of Sparky, Tommy decided to try to make friends with him. Each time Tommy went to Mrs. Caine's house, he would have a dog biscuit ready for Sparky. Although the dog continued to glare, he did accept the biscuits. If nothing else, this made Tommy feel as though he were making some progress toward befriending the dog. Then, Tommy figured, he could work without fear.

Tommy worked three times at the Caine house and Mrs. Caine owed him $6.00. One day, on the way home from school, he decided to stop by to collect his money. He walked by the dog, went up to the front door, and rang the bell. Mrs. Caine wasn't home, so Tommy went back down the walk to go home. He looked at the glaring Sparky, for whom he had no biscuits that day.

"Nice fellow," Tommy said to Sparky and walked by. Suddenly Tommy felt a nudge on the back of his right leg. Turning around, he saw that Sparky had taken hold of the new dress slacks he had bought for himself just two days before. Tommy, frightened, pulled away with all of his might, a move that resulted in a tear about seven inches long and four inches wide on the back of his new slacks. He was very upset, as the slacks had cost him $26.

Tommy telephoned Mrs. Caine that evening and told her what had happened while he was trying to collect his $6.00 for the yard work. Mrs. Caine became infuriated, stating that "sweet Sparky" couldn't have caused any damage and that he must have ripped his pants jumping over a fence somewhere. Tommy told his mother, and both he and his mother filed a claim in Small Claims Court.

Tommy appeared with his mother and told the judge exactly what had happened. Ethel Caine also appeared. Tommy brought the sales slip showing that the pants had been purchased two days before the incident. He also brought the slacks, showing the judge where they had been ripped.

Mrs. Caine denied that her dog could have done it. The judge then asked if Mrs. Caine was present to observe the incident. She said no, but she knows that Sparky doesn't bite, or at least hasn't bitten anybody in over two years. Tommy further told the judge that Mrs. Caine owed him $6.00 and that she refused to pay after he accused her dog of biting him. The judge inquired if this was true, and she said it was.

Result: In the case of *Kathy Williams, as Parent of Tommy Williams* v. *Ethel Caine,* the Judge awarded the full amount of $26 to Tommy plus $6.00 for the work he had done, plus the filing fee.

This case was in the area of negligence. It is used to illustrate a typical case regarding an infant. You should refer to Chapter XI, on negligence, for other rules that may apply.

CHECKLIST FOR CLAIMANT—INFANT

- Check with clerk to see if parent or guardian must sign form.
- If necessary, parent or guardian should go with infant to file claim.
- The same people who file claim should appear in court.
- Bring damaged article to court.
- Bring receipt of purchase or replacement estimate.
- Bring any witnesses who observed the event.

CHECKLIST FOR RESPONDENT

- Supply proof showing lack of negligence (see negligence Checklists for Respondent).

Carol Appleton, as Parent of Jamie Appleton
v.
Silas Warner
CLAIM: Failure to pay infant for services rendered—
money owed paper carrier

Jamie Appleton couldn't wait to turn twelve years old so he could have his own daily morning paper route for the *Sunburst Chronicle.* He was soon to learn, however, that being in busi-

Claims in which a Child Is a Party

ness for yourself is not always easy. In his job, not only would he have to be a good, efficient, and prompt delivery boy, but also he would have to make his rounds each week attempting to collect for his newspapers.

Many of the people on his route paid for the paper directly by being billed at the main office. About half the others would ask Jamie to come to their door each week, collecting. He liked this very much, for most of the people paid on time and he had an opportunity to meet the neighbors. He also from time to time received a tip.

Silas Warner lived alone in a carriage house behind one of the larger homes that Jamie serviced. This delivery was not an easy one. He would have to go all the way to the rear of the property, walk by a barking dog, and leave the paper inside a door. Each week, when he went to collect, Silas would give him a hard time about the exact amount that was owed, or just wouldn't answer the door. Jamie told his district manager that he did not want to deliver the paper to Mr. Warner anymore, but was told to keep trying. At the time the bill was up to $8.60, representing nearly six weeks' delivery and several days profit, Jamie received a notice from the office to stop delivering to Silas Warner. He had moved. That left Jamie with an unpaid bill of $8.60. On his own, Jamie tracked down Silas Warner. He talked to the landlord, who did not know the forwarding address and told Jamie that rent was owed to him as well. Neighbors knew nothing. Finally Jamie located Silas through a letter carrier who helped him track down a forwarding address.

With that information in hand Jamie Appleton and his mother used the Small Claims Court process. When his day in court arrived, in walked Jamie Appleton, his mother, and Silas Warner. Jamie told his story in very clear, orderly terms, indicating that Silas Warner owed him $8.60 and he wasn't going to let him get away. The judge was interested to hear the response the respondent would have for this claim.

A bit embarrassed and uncomfortable, Silas Warner shrugged his shoulders.

Result: In the case of *Carole Appleton, as Parent of Jamie Appleton* v. *Silas Warner,* the decision was given in open court and Silas Warner was directed to turn over to Jamie Appleton the sum of $8.60 plus $4.20 filing fee. Both learned a lesson. Jamie Appleton as a person in business was able to see if he followed through and didn't let somebody get away with taking advantage of him that he would be successful.

Young people do a lot of odd jobs for money. They rake leaves, cut lawns, shovel snow, clean houses, and perform other work that is not considered regular employment. As independent contractors, children should be paid for the fruits of their labors. Small Claims Court assures that they are.

You should refer to the chapter dealing with services performed but not paid to read about additional ways in which to handle the presentation of this type of claim.

CHECKLIST FOR CLAIMANT—INFANT

- Check with clerk to see if parent or guardian must sign form.
- If necessary, parent or guardian should go with infant to file claim.
- The same people who file claim should appear in court.
- Itemized list of work done and hours, together with dates.
- Summary of agreement between the respondent and the infant.
- Any witnesses who observed work.

CHECKLIST FOR RESPONDENT

- See Checklist for Respondent in case of services rendered properly but not paid.

CLAIMS AGAINST INFANTS

As you now know that an infant can bring an action against you, it is equally important to realize that the rules permit you to bring a claim against an infant, as well.

One common example is that of a young person who recklessly operates a car and causes damage to yours. When you start an action against an infant, you name both the infant and the parent. In most cases, the document is served on both. Usually an insurance company will appear on behalf of the respondent in a negligence case. You should use the same procedure in prosecuting the matter as in Chapter XI (see *Tom Sawyer* v. *Richard Dolan*).

In the next chapter, "Claims Against Your Local Government or Governmental Agency," you should note the case of *Sally Sweet, as Parent of Claire Sweet* v. *Lazy River School District and Douglas Clutz*. In that interesting case, infants are represented both on the claimant side and as one of the respondents.

CHAPTER

XIV

Claims Against Your Local Government or Governmental Agency

HAVE YOU EVER suffered a financial loss because your local government failed to fulfill a contract with you or did something that was negligent? You *can* bring a claim in Small Claims Court against your town, village, city, or county government. You may also sue a bridge or tunnel district, a school district, water authority, sewer district, fire department, or local agency. Your local government is subject to the same kinds of claims as individuals.*

The government, for example, operates automobiles, trucks, and police cars and employs people with the same human fallibilities as those of us who are not employed by the government. They can drive automobiles in a careless, reckless and negligent manner; they can do acts that are negligent and cause damage to your property, such as when they pick up your trash and run over your garbage cans; they can also act negligently by failing

---

* Not all municipal suits are appropriate for Small Claims Court. For an excellent discussion of everything you need to know to sue your city, county, or village, see W. Bernard Richland's informative book *You Can Beat City Hall* (New York: Rawson, Wade, 1980).

Claims Against Your Local Government

to fill potholes, fix sidewalks, and put up proper barriers where there are hazardous conditions. If, as a result of the government's negligence, you suffer damage, you should be able to collect from the government. There is one condition, however. You must file what is called a *notice of claim* in all cases of negligence claimed against the government. This is a notice to the government or agency that you file as soon as possible after you become aware that you have a claim. The time period allowed between the event and your filing a notice of claim varies from 3 days in some jurisdictions to 120 days in others. The usual time period is 60 or 90 days. If you don't file the notice, you can't win.

The notice of claim is a document required by state law in any tort (wrongdoing) or negligence case against the government. A notice of claim form can be obtained from the officials at the government or agency office you wish to sue. The purpose of this notice is to allow for an investigation by the municipal body to determine the validity of your claim before a lawsuit is begun. The notice of claim must usually be sworn to in front of a notary public and states your name, address, the time and place of the event in question, and the damages you have suffered. It should either be personally served upon a designated agent for the government or municipal body, or it may be served by registered or certified mail (depending on local rules). For example, if you are filing a claim against a town, you may serve the clerk of the town; a city, the city clerk; a school district, any member of the board, or the secretary to the board. If you ask your public official, he or she will furnish you with guidelines and rules for filing your claim. They are obligated to do so under the law.

Even if you are optimistic that the payment will be voluntary and the public official has assured you that the claim will be paid, the time to file is running from the moment the event occurred. File the notice of claim to preserve your right to bring a legal action against a municipality in court. Act quickly to prevent your claim from being lost in the boondoggle of bureaucratic red tape.

Once you have filed the notice of claim as required, you may then go to your Small Claims Court (if you haven't already been paid). Take proof with you that you have forwarded a notice of claim to the municipal body. Then file your claim with the court clerk just as you would if it were an ordinary negligence case. (For facts that could apply in any negligence case, see Chapter XI.) If your car was hit by a city car or truck, you would follow the same procedure as used in the case of *Tom Sawyer* v. *Richard Dolan*.

All types of claims other than negligence against your local government or governmental agency may be prosecuted in the same manner as if you were suing an individual. They do not require a notice of claim. Contractual obligations, for example, may be enforced just as if you had an agreement with another person that he or she failed to fulfill. Suppose the city was responsible for picking up your trash and failed to do so for several weeks in a row. You have a contract: You pay taxes, they take away refuse.

If you had to hire another trucker to remove your trash at a cost of $25, you would have a claim against the city for breach of contract in that amount.

A sewer district agrees through an implied contract that for payment of the sewage fee portion of your taxes, all of the waste water from your home will be carried away through the trunk sewers of the city. When that system fails and you suffer damage, you may have a claim against the sewer district for a breach of their contract. Such was the case of *David and Lori Pellet* v. *Metro City Sewage District*.

David and Lori Pellet v. Metro City Sewage District
CLAIM: Damage for sewage backup

David and Lori Pellet had lived in their house for forty-two years and had never had any difficulty with their sewer lines. They lived in one of eight houses on a dead-end street. In June, a heavy storm dumped five inches of rain in a three-hour period. Shortly after the rain stopped, the Pellets detected a pungent odor coming from their basement. Mr. Pellet went down and saw sewage backing up through the lavatory. His cellar floor was covered with nearly two feet of sewage, as was the bottom of the furnace and many items that were stored in the basement.

He immediately contacted personnel at the sewage district office, who quickly sent a cleanup crew. The supervisor of the crew said that there must have been something wrong with Mr. Pellet's line to cause the problem. Soon, other neighbors notified the sewer district that they had the same difficulty. The district superintendent was then overheard by a neighbor saying there was some problem with construction on North Street, the main road that led to the Pellets' street. The crew temporarily took care of the problem and assured Mr. Pellet that it would not happen again.

Mr. Pellet decided to do some investigating. He talked to construction crews working on the main sewer line on North Street and learned that a temporary line was put in that was two feet higher than the normal sewer line. He also asked one of his neighbors, John Laraby, a former sanitation engineer, to go with him to inspect the new line, which had not yet been covered with dirt. Laraby immediately noticed that the pipe was two feet higher than it should be. He also knew that sometimes during heavy rains the sewers become plugged because the storm rain water in this district drains into the same sewer as the sanitary waste. Laraby and Mr. Pellet both got copies of sewer maps from the sanitation department to verify their belief. Mr. Pellet then made a claim to the city by notifying them that the backed-up sewer had damaged his furnace, which required $372 to repair. It also damaged Christmas ornaments and other items stored on the basement floor. Additional cleanup costs brought the total amount to $772. The city told Mr. Pellet that the claim would not be paid, so he took the matter to Small Claims Court.

In Small Claims Court, Mr. Pellet indicated that a temporary pipe caused the problem. He showed, by using maps and examining the city engineer whom he had subpoenaed, that the sewage was supposed to flow down to the end of his street and through the main sewer on North Street. This couldn't happen, Mr. Pellet said, because the main sewer on North Street was higher than the drain from his street. All the water and sewage from the main artery went back down the short residential street and into the basements of houses. Mr. Pellet then presented photographs of his basement, together with estimates of the cost of repair. The furnace had to be completely cleaned and sanitized so that the smell would not circulate throughout the entire house.

The sewer district's defense was the heavy rain. The attorney who represented the district said if they paid this claim, they would have to pay literally thousands of dollars in claims, and they believed their only obligation was to clean up the houses, not to pay for additional damages.

Result: In the case of *David and Lori Pellet* v. *Metro City Sewage District,* the judge awarded payment in full to the claimants. In this case, Mr. Pellet did some good detective work and found that the cause of the sewage backup was poor engineering on the part of the city.

This action was brought as a contract claim because the sewage district, in accepting payment of taxes, contracts to have the sewage flow away from people's houses and not back into them. It is an implied public contract.

And the defense of heavy rain? All wet, ruled the judge.

Many other claims may be made against your city. Bill

Claims Against Your Local Government

Goldman was driving his new subcompact car to work. While on a city street, he suddenly heard a loud noise and felt as if his entire car had fallen into a crater. As he bounced back out of it, he pulled over to the side of the road and found that both tires on the right side had been flattened. He turned around to find that he had driven into the largest pothole he had ever seen. He called his car dealer and had the car towed away and fully checked for damage. He later paid a bill for two tires and a broken shock absorber. His total bill was $175, including towing. He was discussing this at work when a colleague, Vince Welch, told him that he went into the same pothole three days before and wrote a letter notifying the city of the problem. Bill Goldman then attempted unsuccessfully to collect from the city. He gave up, filed a notice of claim within the week, and a week later brought an action in Small Claims Court. After proving his case as to the amount of damage and showing that the city had received the proper prior notice of the defective condition, the court gave him the award in full.

The city is negligent if a dangerous condition is not repaired. There is a precedent, however, that a city must have prior notice of the condition before they can be held liable. If you don't happen to run into another person who has notified the municipality of the dangerous condition and you suffer a loss, you can, through the various freedom of information laws, discover whether there had been any notice by another person. If there hasn't been, you are out of luck. Be sure to put the city on notice, though. You may help the next unfortunate driver.

Sally Sweet, as Parent of Claire Sweet
v.
Lazy River School District and Douglas Clutz

CLAIM: Negligence on behalf of school district—
improper supervision

Claire Street and Douglas Clutz were both eighth-graders at the Lincoln Junior High School, where the school's Musical Guild was producing a light operetta as an after-school activity. Some of the youngsters were selected to sing in the operetta; others could participate by helping in painting scenery.

One winter afternoon, both Claire Sweet and Doug Clutz volunteered to paint scenery. Claire was seated on the floor with her friends, carefully sketching a landscape of trees and bright flowers.

Mr. Gilbert, the teacher, took two of the boys to the art room to carry paints and brushes. Doug Clutz was carrying two pails of paint, which had been opened in the art room and stirred to the proper consistency.

After he carefully carried them down to the stage area, he attempted to lift them to a work bench two feet from where Claire Sweet was seated on the floor. Suddenly, for some unknown reason, the top pail of orange paint fell and spilled all over Claire; her hair, her clothes, and the scenery she was painting turned orange.

Mr. Gilbert, who was just a few feet away, observed the accident and helped her clean up. Fortunately, the paint had a water base and was readily washed out of her hair.

Just the day before, Claire had purchased her first new winter dress coat, which she was wearing at the time of the accident. Since it was after school on a cold day, the heat was turned down, and she needed it to keep warm.

When Claire arrived home, her mother, Sally (who was furious), was unable to clean the bright orange paint off the new coat. All attempts at dry-cleaning or laundering failed. Claire was proud of her first new winter coat, which now appeared doomed. Mrs. Sweet had little money and was supporting five other children. She contacted the school's principal and asked that the school replace the coat. He told her no, it was merely an accident and that "accidents can happen."

The cost of the new coat was $96.50. Mrs. Sweet filed a notice of claim against the school district, as is required in a negligence case against a municipality. The negligence, she claimed, arose from improper supervision of the students by Mr. Gilbert. Doug Clutz, she claimed, was also being sued for negligence because Sally Sweet felt he had not exercised proper care.

The Sweets then filed their claim in Small Claims Court against both the school district and Doug Clutz and his father, Joe Clutz. (A minor can be sued only by putting a parent or guardian on notice. See Chapter XIII.)

At the time of the hearing, Mrs. Sweet, Claire, Mr. Clutz, Doug, and representatives from the school district, including Mr. Gilbert, the teacher, and Averill Starch, a school board representative, appeared.

Claire contended through her mother's testimony that the accident wouldn't have happened if the after-school activity had been properly supervised. The school should not have permitted an eighth-grader to carry paint that could spill, she said.

Mr. Gilbert indicated that these boys and girls are old enough to take care of themselves and that he had supervised them properly throughout the activity. Mr. Gilbert, in asking Doug to carry paint in the manner he did, could not have foreseen the resulting damage to Claire's coat. Therefore, the school was not negligent.

Averill Starch, on behalf of the school district, said that the school was not liable and would be unable to pay anything because it would set an expensive precedent. Doug Clutz apologized profusely for the incident, saying he didn't know what caused it and *he* certainly could not have foreseen the result.

The judge then stopped the hearing. He saw that Claire and Sally Sweet had little money and believed that the school district and Doug Clutz with his father, Joe, might somehow make some contribution toward a new coat.

The judge ruled in front of the parties that there was no legal liability on behalf of either Doug Clutz or the Lazy River School District to make payment. He ruled that the paint spill was an unfortunate accident, the result of which was unforeseen rather than intentional, and that Lazy River School District had provided proper supervision.

The judge then called all parties forward and said he felt that Lazy River School District, having a budget of $150 million, must have a fund someplace to come up with less than $100 to reimburse the young claimant for the damage to her coat.

Mr. Starch said that would be very poor precedent, but if the judge made it a strong suggestion in writing, he would convince the Board of Education to contribute something toward it.

Doug Clutz' father, Joe, then said, "I feel very badly about this girl and would be willing to pay one half of her damage if the school district would pay the other half."

Starch thought that was a good idea.

So did Claire Sweet and her mother.

The judge then marked the case as settled.

Result: In the case of *Sally Sweet, as Parent of Claire Sweet* v. *Lazy River School District and Douglas Clutz,* the case was settled after hearing. (As in this case, a negligence action can be brought against a school district, providing that a notice of claim is filed on time.) Here the only legal theory upon which the Sweet family could proceed was improper supervision by the school district. They would have had to prove that Mr. Gilbert did something improper by his failure to supervise the children; that the children had gotten out of hand; or that he could have foreseen damage to the coat of Claire Sweet by his actions. It's difficult to prove these circumstances.

The only other possibility would be to show that young Doug knew the result of his act of carrying the cans of paint or that he intentionally spilled paint on a fellow student. The fair result in this case could have been achieved only after a hearing with the judge trying to bring the parties together in a fair solution. Often, in a case such as this, conscience will be the factor that makes the parties agree to some payment, even though they are not legally liable.

Checklist for Claimant Bringing Action Against Municipality

- File notice of claim with municipal agency as required by law.
- Bring proof of service of notice of claim together with a copy to court.
- Estimates of damage.
- Photographs showing damaged goods.
- Witnesses who have experienced the same problem or witnessed the difficulty.
- Subpoena expert witnesses, if necessary.

(Follow other checklists for specific nature of claim.)

CHAPTER

XV

Intentional Damage and Missing Goods—Lost or Stolen

Now that you've learned about contract disputes, negligence, improper services, and defective products, you're well informed on many of the unintentionally harmful areas for which you can be reimbursed through Small Claims Court.

This chapter deals with the person who intentionally struck you, causing you harm; or the one who vandalized your property "just for fun." In these cases, the damage or loss was intentional. You were intentionally hit; your property was intentionally damaged; or you were intentionally robbed or deprived of your property.

Although most cases involving intentional damage and missing goods (theft) are prosecuted in other courts, it is sometimes not possible to prosecute the person responsible for your intentional injury, damage, or loss because of some legal problem. Or you may not wish to go through a long, complicated, and expensive court procedure, since there is another way to be compensated for your loss.

CLAIMS FOR INJURY OR DAMAGE SUFFERED FROM INTENTIONAL ACTS

Has a friend or stranger ever caused damage to your property? The reason that the damage is caused is often unknown, but it appears there was a definite intent by the person who caused the damage. Perhaps you woke up one morning and found that the antenna on your automobile had been snapped off; or that your mailbox had been toppled over; or a window had been broken. If you can prove who caused the damage, you can then contact the person to try to receive compensation.

As in all other claims, you should obtain an estimate for the cost of repair of the item that was damaged. It is a good idea to try to talk to the person who caused the damage to find out if they intend to pay you. During that conversation, you may be able to obtain some kind of an admission that the damage was caused by him or her. If you cannot resolve the dispute and the damage is not significant enough to warrant an arrest, then you may go to Small Claims Court.

This occurred in the case of *Scott Wilde* v. *Carl Cranke.*

Scott Wilde v. *Carl Cranke*
CLAIM: Damage to snowmobile

Scott Wilde, an avid snowmobiler, was a volunteer providing emergency relief for people stranded during snowstorms. Each year the local police department furnished him with a list of people who might have difficulty getting out during heavy snows. Since they had no telephones, Scott's assignment was to check on their well-being. He would see that they got anything they needed, but most importantly, his presence gave them a sense of security.

With his own funds, Scott had purchased a new snowmobile with which to make his rounds. He carried various foodstuffs, medical supplies, and other emergency materials with him.

After eighteen inches of snow had fallen, Scott received word that a couple may have been stranded at the end of Liberty Street. The plows had been unable to keep the street open, as the snow had fallen too fast. Scott went to the couple's home, but on the way, he met Carl Cranke.

Cranke was a feisty old man who had been shoveling his driveway. Five minutes before he first saw Scott Wilde, four snowmobiles had come racing down his street and had nearly run him over.

Cranke was enraged. The next snowmobile to come by that evening was Scott Wilde's. As Scott slowly proceeded down the street with his headlight on, Cranke decided he was going to take care of the problem. He raised his shovel and threw it, smashing the snowmobile's deck, breaking the windshield, and shattering the hood into many pieces. Wilde contacted the police and they all discussed it with Cranke. Because of Wilde's desire to help elderly people, he had compassion for Cranke's problem and decided not to have the elderly man arrested. Scott merely wanted to be reimbursed $625 for the damage to his equipment.

Scott Wilde appeared in Small Claims Court and told the judge that he had never been on Liberty Street before and was just driving his snowmobile to the end of the street to help the elderly couple. Carl Cranke then related that he knew that Scott had been down the street before because he saw lights just like Scott's on four other snowmobiles that had nearly run him over.

The judge then asked Cranke how he knew that this was the same snowmobile that nearly struck him and he replied, "Well, they all look alike."

Scott presented the estimates for repair of his snowmobile together with pieces of the shattered hood. The estimates were in proper form, together with photographs.

Result: In the case of *Scott Wilde* v. *Carl Cranke*, decision was granted in favor of the claimant for the amount of $625.

Intentional Damage and Missing Goods—Lost or Stolen

Scott was the victim of a person's impulsive anger. Although Carl Cranke felt he was the victim, since he almost got injured by other snowmobiles, his action only made his predicament worse. It is not only unlawful (in criminal codes) in every state to cause damage to another person or another person's property intentionally, it is also irrational. Cranke's reaction of anger and retaliation was destructive. He was lucky that the snowmobile he struck belonged to Scott Wilde, someone of maturity and good judgment.

Carl Cranke's action differs from negligence as defined in Chapter XI. Cranke intended his act to result in damage to either Scott Wilde or his snowmobile. The simplest distinction is that an act can be considered negligent only when the result is an unintended (but normally avoidable) accident. In that type of case, the degree of negligence must be considered to see if there is any negligence by the person making the claim, in which case the amount awarded may be reduced. In the area of an intentional striking, only the conduct of the person who acts with intent is considered. He will be fully responsible for his acts.

Another type of action involving intentional harm to others is assault. In assault cases the claimant brings a claim for reimbursement of out-of-pocket medical expenses, lost wages that resulted from the striking, and any other actual expenses. The claimant may not sue to be compensated for pain, suffering, or inconvenience in Small Claims Court, but can pursue that remedy in another court. Sometimes assault cases are heard in Small Claims Court because the victim decided not to prosecute the matter in Criminal Court. At other times, they are heard because the criminal action was dismissed in a higher court. A much higher burden of proof is required in a criminal case than in a civil case. In order to find a person guilty in a criminal case, it must be proven "beyond a reasonable doubt." A civil case requires only that a preponderance of the evidence show that the claim is valid. In simpler terms, this means that the scales must tip at least ever so slightly in favor of the claimant in Small Claims Court.

The best alternatives to both Criminal Court and Small Claims Court for intentional assaults are the centers for dispute settlements provided in most cities. These centers offer efficient, informal, and just decisions through a process of mediation or arbitration. Both parties, however, must agree to use the centers rather than the courts.

Checklist for Claimant

- Estimate of repair of item damaged.
- If possible, bring damaged item to court.
- Police report and presentation of any witnesses.
- Give any incriminating statements made by respondent to you or the police.
- Photographs of damage.
- Medical reports, if appropriate.
- Medical bills.
- Employer's statement of lost wages.
- Letter from doctor indicating time was necessarily lost from work.

Checklist for Respondent

- Present witnesses who will show that the claim is without merit.

MISSING GOODS

If you have ever entrusted another person with an item that has not been returned to you, you might immediately think it was stolen. Since items don't just disappear, it is possible that the other person has decided to keep your goods and has benefited from their use. If you can't find the thief, you try to find

Intentional Damage and Missing Goods—Lost or Stolen 189

the person who may be liable because he or she should have guarded the goods to prevent the theft. This was the claim of Terry Rogers.

Terry Rogers v. Frank's Laundromat
CLAIM: Clothing missing from laundromat

The washer in the Rogers' household had just been pronounced dead by a qualified repairman. Since they couldn't afford a new one right away, Terry Rogers and his wife decided that they would use the laundromat around the corner until they had saved enough money to buy a new washer. Terry took a large load of wash to Frank's Laundromat. He put the laundry in the washer, placed the coins in the slot, put the proper amount of soap in, and turned on the washer.

There was no attendant on duty. A sign indicated that the laundromat would close at 9:00 P.M. Another sign on the property indicated that the owner of the laundromat would not be responsible for lost or stolen items. When Terry came back to the laundromat at 8:35 P.M., the doors were locked and it appeared the laundromat was closed. Terry, assuming that his wash was safely locked inside, went home.

The next morning, at nine o'clock, he called the proprietor, Frank Spinelli. Frank checked the machines, and found that the clothes were no longer there. That evening, at eight-thirty, Terry went back to the laundromat and talked to Joe Brown, who was cleaning up. He told Terry that he did close early the night before because there was nobody in the laundromat and no machines were then operating. He said he did remember that one of the machines had a load of laundry in it, but that often happens and people come back the next day.

Terry Rogers and his wife itemized all of the goods that were missing and replaced them, obtaining receipts in the amount of $148.75, including tax. Rogers requested that Frank's Laundromat reimburse him for all of the missing goods inasmuch as it closed early. Frank Spinelli said that he didn't have any attendants in the laundromat and refused to pay, as it was the responsibility of the person who used the machines to sit and watch their clothing.

Terry Rogers brought a claim to Small Claims Court. He and his wife appeared with several receipts showing replacement costs for the missing goods, including both children's and adult's clothes, dishcloths, towels, and undergarments. He subpoenaed Joe Brown, the maintenance man. Frank Spinelli also appeared.

Terry Rogers stated that he saw the sign that said the laundromat would be open until 9:00 P.M., as well as the sign that said the owner would not be responsible for lost or stolen goods. Rogers relied on the fact, however, that the laundromat would stay open until the time when he could pick up the clothes.

Frank Spinelli stated that he felt very sorry for Rogers and his family, but that thefts could and often do occur at a laundromat. He added that people normally come into his establishment, which is unattended, and wait for their laundry to be completed. At no time does any employee of his participate in doing the laundry, he said, noting that this differs from some other laundromats. It is the responsibility of the owner of the clothing not only to do the wash, but to remove it as well, he said. The only service that is provided by Frank's Laundromat is the use of the machines.

Upon cross-examination, Frank Spinelli asked Terry Rogers if he saw the sign indicating that Frank did not accept any responsibility for lost or stolen goods, and Terry said yes, he had seen the sign. The cleaning man, Joe Brown (who was subpoenaed by Rogers), stated that he closed about twenty-five minutes early that evening because nobody was in the laundromat and no machines were operating. He added that if somebody had come in to do their wash that late, they could not have completed a full cycle by the time the laundromat was due to close.

Intentional Damage and Missing Goods—Lost or Stolen 191

Spinelli had given Joe Brown permission to lock the doors and close early.

Result: In the case of *Terry Rogers* v. *Frank's Laundromat*, the judge ruled no cause for action. While the court felt very sorry for Terry Rogers and his family, the judge relied on the fact that Frank's Laundromat only provided use of the machines and at no time guaranteed that they would safeguard clothing left in the washers and dryers. To the contrary, they expressly limited their liability by the sign stating that they would not be responsible for such loss due to theft.

During the course of the testimony, Spinelli indicated that theft frequently occurs in laundromats. If he were to be responsible for all the thefts, he would not be able to remain in business. He encouraged people to remain with their clothes until the wash is finished. If an attendant were present, then the responsibility would have shifted to the owner of the laundromat. That was not the case here, however.

Another type of lost-goods nightmare that breathes fear into the hearts of travelers is loss of luggage. Because of the speed of baggage handling and the high volume involved, the most frequent incidents involve baggage lost by airlines. Your baggage may have been routed one way while you traveled another, or, in fact, it may have been stolen.

Federal regulations limit an airline's maximum liability to $750 per piece of luggage, unless you insured against loss for a higher amount. Usually the airlines are courteous and prompt in either finding your baggage or paying the claim. On occasion, however, you may become frustrated and angry with the lack of service. In that case you may bring an action in Small Claims Court in any jurisdiction in which the airline does business. Be sure you make a prompt report of the loss and can document your claim fully.

Jack Kilder v. Center City Motors
CLAIM: Missing tire

Two years before this action in Small Claims Court, Mr. Kilder purchased a new automobile from Center City Motors. Each time something went wrong with the car, he brought it back for repair. The station wagon held a spare tire in a special inside compartment. The spare tire was not readily visible unless one were to open the compartment and look for it. Jack's wife was the only person who ever noticed the tire. She checked that it had air in it whenever she cleaned the car's interior.

One day, Mr. Kilder took his car to Center City Motors for an oil change. Two months later, while the couple was preparing for their summer vacation, Mrs. Kilder checked the spare tire while she was cleaning the interior of the car. She opened up the compartment and found it was empty. Mr. Kilder deduced that the spare was taken when the car was at Center City Motors for service and took the matter to Small Claims Court. When asked by the judge if there were any proof that Center City Motors was responsible for his missing tire, Mr. Kilder said that he had never given the keys to anyone else. It was obvious to him that Center City Motors was the culprit.

Bob Swift, the oil-change and grease mechanic for Center City Motors, testified that when he changed the oil, he checked all four tires as well as the spare in the compartment. He said that if there had been no spare, he would have made an immediate report, a procedure required at Center City Motors. He said he performed approximately fifteen oil changes and lubrications per day and had no time to remove tires unless they needed repair.

Result: In the case of *Jack Kilder* v. *Center City Motors,* the judge ruled no cause for action. In this case, the claimant had only a suspicion and no proof that the respondent was responsible for the missing tire. The judge believed that any

Intentional Damage and Missing Goods—Lost or Stolen

number of things could have happened to the tire during the two-month time lapse in this case.

In the case of missing goods, it is not required that a case be proven beyond a reasonable doubt (as in a criminal prosecution), but merely that the evidence indicate that it is substantially likely that the event occurred and that the respondent is responsible for it. Some proof must justify an accusation or claim.

The court heard another case two weeks later involving similar facts. Sue Eagle claimed she took her car to the service station to have some work done with the tail-light housing. This required that the trunk be opened. Miss Eagle claimed that the day before she took the car to the service station, she was picking up a friend at the airport and saw her spare tire in the trunk. On the way home from the service station, she got a flat tire, opened the trunk, and found that the spare tire and wheel were missing. The only person who had access to the trunk in that short period of time was the service-station attendant. Sue Eagle brought an action in Small Claims Court and was successful.

You can see the difference between the Kilder and Eagle cases. The limited time period in Miss Eagle's case removed most of the speculation that someone other than the service-station attendant could have taken the tire.

Checklist for Claimant

- Any document, such as a receipt, indicating your contact with the respondent.
- Photograph or photographs of item or items claimed to be missing, if possible.
- Itemized list of missing goods.
- Itemized replacement value of missing goods—at least two estimates, unless you have the actual receipt of purchase.
- Any police report or eyewitnesses' statements.
- You may subpoena the person you believe was responsible for the care of your missing goods (as did Terry Rogers).

Checklist for Respondent

- State what warning was given about your lack of responsibility for lost items.
- State what care you took to insure there was no loss or theft.
- Present witnesses who had care and custody of items.
- Present your own estimates of repair or replacement.

Summary

Now you know everything you need to know about Small Claims Court. The procedures, as set out in Part One of this book, have given you step-by-step guidelines to follow. You now know if you have a valid claim and how to take it to court. You no longer have to walk around grumbling that another person has taken advantage of you.

Now that you have read these cases you have a feeling for the way things are done in Small Claims Court. You can use the judge's rationale to your advantage in presenting your own claims or defending those brought against you.

Just be sure to remember one thing: Make your presentation honest and accurate and you will find that you *can* win *BIG* in Small Claims Court!

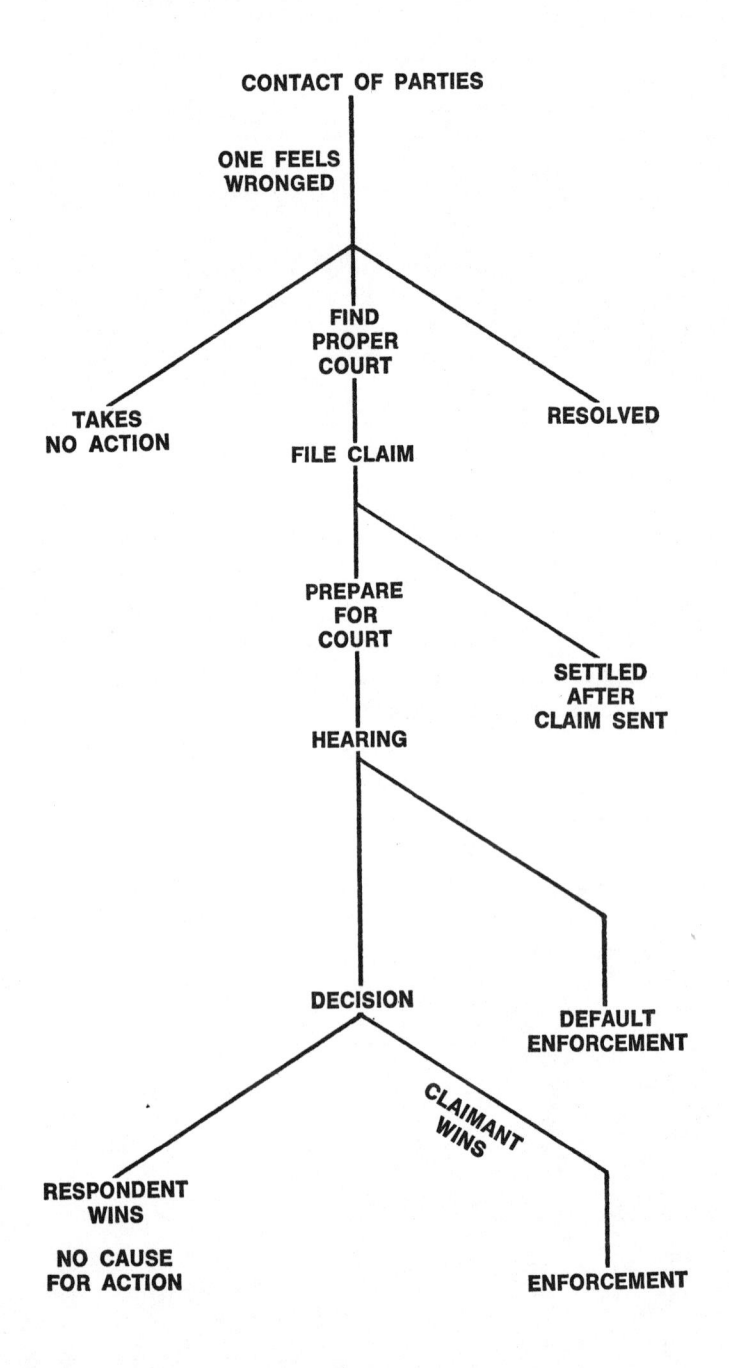

Appendix A: Small Claims Court Flow Chart

```
                    CONTACT OF PARTIES
                            |
                      ONE FEELS
                       WRONGED
                       /   |   \
                      /    |    \
                     /   FIND    \
                    /   PROPER    \
                   /     COURT     \
                  /       |         \
             TAKES        |        RESOLVED
           NO ACTION   FILE CLAIM
                          |
                          |
                      PREPARE
                        FOR
                       COURT       \
                          |         \
                          |        SETTLED
                          |         AFTER
                       HEARING   CLAIM SENT
                          |
                          |
                          |
                          |
                       DECISION      \
                        /    \     DEFAULT
                       /      \   ENFORCEMENT
                      /        \
                     /      CLAIMANT
                    /         WINS
              RESPONDENT
                WINS
              NO CAUSE
             FOR ACTION              ENFORCEMENT
```

Appendix B: Table of Variations of Small Claims Courts by State

As you have read throughout this book, there are minor variations from state to state in the general rules and procedures of Small Claims Courts. They vary not only from state to state, but also within each state. Precise information may be obtained only by contacting your local Small Claims Court clerk.

In the preparation of this book, we have contacted several courts in each state to verify information listed. Questions in our survey revealed that all of the states have informal procedures; that the time from filing of a claim to a hearing is generally thirty days, although there is some variance, from two weeks up to four months. We further found that lawyers are allowed in most Small Claims Courts (exceptions noted), but rarely participate in the proceedings. The length of hearings varies from ten minutes to an hour, but generally averages twenty minutes.

Only categories in which there are some key variations are listed, specifically, the name of each court and a suggestion as to how to look it up in the phone book in your area; the location where you should file your claim; and the maximum-claim limit.

Legislation is pending in several states to raise the amount for which you can sue.

Alabama
Name of court: District Court, located in each county; listed under county or state
Venue: The respondent must reside or do business within the jurisdiction of the court
Claim limit: $500

Alaska
Name of court: District Court; listed under state of Alaska, District Court, Small Claims
Venue: The respondent must reside within the jurisdiction of the court
Claim limit: $2,000

Arizona
Name of court: County Court, Small Claims Part, justice of the peace; listed under the name of your county. In some rural areas, would be listed under Justice Court in the name of the local community
Venue: The respondent must reside within the jurisdiction of the court
Claim limit: $2,500

Arkansas
Name of court: County Court or Municipal Court; listed under the name of the county
Venue: Either the respondent must reside within the jurisdiction of the court, or the action must have taken place within the jurisdiction of the court
Claim limit: Property damage, $100
Other claims, $300

California
Name of court: Municipal Court; listed under local government or county, Municipal or Justice Court
Venue: Either the respondent must reside within the jurisdiction of the court, or the action must have taken place within the jurisdiction of the court.
Claim limit: $750 ($1,500 in jurisdiction of San Bernardino [Chino Division], East Los Angeles, West Orange County, Fresno, Compton, and Oakland-Piedmont)
Note: Lawyers not allowed

Colorado
Name of court: County Court, Small Claims Division; listed under the name of the county
Venue: Either the respondent must reside within the jurisdiction of the court, or do business within the jurisdiction of the court
Claim limit: $500 (legislation pending to raise limit to $1,000)
Note: The respondent may bring an attorney only if the claimant has brought an attorney

Connecticut
Name of court: Superior Court, twenty-one geographical districts statewide; listed under state of Connecticut, Superior Court

Table of Variations of Small Claims Courts by State

Venue: The respondent must reside within the jurisdiction of the court
Claim limit: $750

Delaware

Name of court: Justice of the Peace Court; listed under the state of Delaware
Venue: Action must have occurred within the jurisdiction of the court
Claim limit: $1,500

District of Columbia

Name of court: District Court; listed under District of Columbia
Venue: Either the respondent must reside within the jurisdiction of the court, or the action must have occurred within the jurisdiction of the court
Claim limit: $750

Florida

Name of court: County Court, Civil Division; listed under the name of the county
Venue: Either the respondent must reside or do business within the jurisdiction of the court, or the action must have occurred within the jurisdiction of the court
Claim limit: $1,500

Georgia

Name of court: State Court, Small Claims Division in large cities; Justice of the Peace Court in rural counties
Venue: The respondent must reside within the jurisdiction of the court
Claim limit: Large cities, $299.99
  Rural areas (Justice of the Peace Courts), $200
Note: Lawyers are not allowed

Hawaii

Name of court: District Court; listed under state of Hawaii, Judiciary Department
Venue: The respondent must reside or do business within the jurisdiction of the court
Claim limit: $1,000
Note: Lawyers are not allowed for security deposit cases

Idaho
Name of court: County Court within judicial districts; listed under the name of the county, Magistrate Division, county district
Venue: The respondent must reside or do business within the jurisdiction of the court
Claim limit: $1,000
Note: Lawyers are not allowed

Illinois
Name of court: In Chicago, Municipal District Court; listed under city of Chicago; otherwise, County Court; listed under name of county
Venue: Either the respondent must reside within the jurisdiction of the court, or the action must have taken place within the jurisdiction of the court
Claim limit: Chicago, $1,000; under $500, the plaintiff must not be represented by an attorney; for claims between $500 and $1,000, either side may be represented by an attorney. Outlying areas, $2,500

Indiana
Name of court: County Court, Small Claims Division; Justice Courts in rural counties, listed under name of county
Venue: Either the respondent must reside within the jurisdiction of the court, or the action must have taken place within the jurisdiction of the court
Claim limit: $1,500

Iowa
Name of court: District Court; listed under state of Iowa, District Court, Small Claims Division
Venue: Action must have occurred within the jurisdiction of the court
Claim limit: $1,000

Kansas
Name of court: District Court, Limited Actions Division in certain areas; otherwise, District Court, listed under name of county
Venue: The respondent must reside within the jurisdiction of the court
Claim limit: $500

Table of Variations of Small Claims Courts by State

Kentucky
Name of court: District Court, Small Claims Division; listed under state of Kentucky, Government Offices, Small Claims
Venue: The respondent must reside within the jurisdiction of the court
Claim limit: $1,000

Louisiana
Name of court: City Court or Parish Court; listed under Government section, City Court, Small Claims Division
Venue: The respondent must reside within the jurisdiction of the court
Claim limit: $750

Maine
Name of court: District Court; listed under state of Maine, District Court, Small Claims
Venue: Either the respondent must reside within the jurisdiction of the court, or the action must have occurred within the jurisdiction of the court
Claim limit: $800

Maryland
Name of court: District Court; listed under state of Maryland or county, Civil Division, Small Claims
Venue: Either the respondent must reside within the jurisdiction of the court, or the action must have occurred within the jurisdiction of the court
Claim limit: $500

Massachusetts
Name of court: Municipal Court in urban areas; otherwise, District Court statewide; listed under local government, Municipal Court, or state of Massachusetts, District Court
Venue: The respondent must reside within the jurisdiction of the court
Claim limit: Varies, but generally $750 (legislation is pending to raise the limit to $1,200)

Michigan
Name of court: District Court; listed under state of Michigan, District Court, Civil Division

Venue: The respondent must reside within the jurisdiction of the court
Claim limit: Detroit, $300
Elsewhere, $600

Minnesota
Name of court: In Minneapolis, County Court, Municipal Division, Small Claims; listed under name of county. Statewide, Municipal Court; listed under name of county
Venue: The respondent must reside within the jurisdiction of the court
Claim limit: $1,000

Mississippi
Name of court: Justice Court; listed under local municipality or local justice of the peace
Venue: The respondent must reside within the jurisdiction of the court
Claim limit: $500

Missouri
Name of court: County Court; listed under name of county
Venue: Either the respondent must reside within the jurisdiction of the court, or the action must have occurred within the jurisdiction of the court
Claim limit: $500

Montana
Name of court: Justice of the Peace Court; listed under County Government, Justice Court, or by contacting specific justice of the peace
Venue: The respondent must reside within the jurisdiction of the court or do business within the jurisdiction of the court
Claim limit: $750

Nebraska
Name of court: Municipal Court, County Court; listed under city or county
Venue: Action must have occurred within the jurisdiction of the court
Claim limit: $1,000

Table of Variations of Small Claims Courts by State

Nevada
Name of court: Justice Court; listed under state or county, Justice Court, Small Claims
Venue: The respondent must reside within the jurisdiction of the court
Claim limit: $750

New Hampshire
Name of court: District Court; listed under name of city
Venue: Either the respondent must reside within the jurisdiction of the court, or the action must have occurred within the jurisdiction of the court
Claim limit: $500

New Jersey
Name of court: District Court, a division of County Court; listed under name of county
Venue: The respondent must reside within the jurisdiction of the court
Claim limit: $500

New Mexico
Name of court: Metropolitan Court, Civil Division; in outlying areas, may be Magistrates Court; listed under name of county or state
Venue: Either the respondent must reside within the jurisdiction of the Court, or the action must have occurred within the jurisdiction of the court
Claim limit: $5,000

New York
Name of court: City Court, Town Court, Village Court, or District Court, depending on location; listed under local government
Venue: The respondent must reside or do business within the jurisdiction of the court
Claim limit: $1,500

North Carolina
Name of court: Superior Court, Small Claims Division; listed under the name of the state
Venue: The respondent must reside within the jurisdiction of the court
Claim limit: $800

North Dakota

Name of court: County Court, Small Claims Division; listed under name of county
Venue: The respondent must reside within the jurisdiction of the court
Claim limit: $1,000

Ohio

Name of court: Municipal County Court in cities; in other areas, County District Court; listed under name of city or county, Small Claims Division
Venue: The respondent must reside within the jurisdiction of the court
Claim limit: $500

Oklahoma

Name of court: County Court, Small Claims Division; listed under name of county
Venue: Either the respondent must reside within the jurisdiction of the court, or the action must have occurred within the jurisdiction of the court
Claim limit: $600

Oregon

Name of court: District Court or Justice Court, Small Claims Department; listed under name of county or local government
Venue: Action must have occurred within the jurisdiction of the court
Claim limit: $700
Note: Attorneys are not allowed

Pennsylvania

Name of court: Municipal Court, Small Claims Branch in Philadelphia; in remainder of state, either County Court or Justice of the Peace Court; listed under local municipality or County Court, Small Claims Division
Venue: Either the respondent must reside within the jurisdiction of the court, or the action must have occurred within the jurisdiction of the court
Claim limit: Philadelphia, $1,000
　Elsewhere, $2,000

Table of Variations of Small Claims Courts by State

Rhode Island
Name of court: State District Court; listed under name of state or county
Venue: The respondent must reside within the jurisdiction of the court
Claim limit: $500

South Carolina
Name of court: Magistrates Court; listed under County Government
Venue: The respondent must reside within the jurisdiction of the court
Claim limit: $1,000 (legislation is pending to raise the limit to $2,500)

South Dakota
Name of court: Circuit Court, Magistrates Division; listed under state or county, Circuit Court, and also magistrate by name
Venue: The respondent must reside within the jurisdiction of the court
Claim limit: $2,000

Tennessee
Name of court: County Court, General Sessions Court; also may be Justice of the Peace Court; listed under name of county, General Sessions Court, Civil Division
Venue: The respondent must reside within the jurisdiction of the court
Claim limit: Recovery of unpaid loan for purchase of personal property, $10,000
All other actions, $5,000

Texas
Name of court: Justice of the Peace Court; listed under local municipality, Justice of the Peace Court, Small Claims Division
Venue: The respondent must reside within the jurisdiction of the court
Claim limit: $150 (legislation is pending to raise the limit)
Labor performed or wages, $200

Utah
Name of court: Circuit Court, Small Claims Division; listed under City Government, Circuit Court, or local municipality, Small Claims Division

Venue: Either the respondent must reside within the jurisdiction of the court, or the action must have occurred within the jurisdiction of the court
Claim limit: $400 (legislation is pending to raise the limit to $1,000)
Note: Lawyers are not allowed

Vermont
Name of court: District Court; listed under state of Vermont, District Court
Venue: The respondent must reside within the jurisdiction of the court, or the action must have occurred within the jurisdiction of the court
Claim limit: $500

Virginia
Name of court: District Court; listed under the name of the state or county, Claim Division
Venue: Either the respondent must reside or do business within the jurisdiction of the court, or the action must have occurred within the jurisdiction of the court
Claim limit: $5,000

Washington
Name of court: County District Court (and Justice Court in some areas); listed under name of county, District Court (or Justice Court)
Venue: The respondent must reside within the jurisdiction of the court
Claim limit: $500

West Virginia
Name of court: Magistrates Court, Small Claims; listed under name of county or also under name of judge for Magistrates Court
Venue: The respondent must reside within the jurisdiction of the court
Claim limit: $1,500

Wisconsin
Name of court: Circuit Court; listed under County Government, Small Claims
Venue: The respondent must reside within the jurisdiction of the court
Claim limit: $1,000

Table of Variations of Small Claims Courts by State

Wyoming

Name of court: County Court and Justice of the Peace Court; listed under name of county, Small Claims, or specific justice of the peace

Venue: Action must have occurred within the jurisdiction of the court

Claim limit: $750

GLOSSARY OF TERMS

Admission—words said against the interest of the speaker.

Appeal—the process by which the losing party asks a higher court to review the case and modify or reverse the decision of the original court. In Small Claims Court cases, this review is based on the stenographer's notes, not on a second court appearance.

Arbitrator—a person appointed by a judge of Small Claims Court who acts in his or her place, hearing the case and rendering a decision. This person is not a judge, but may be a lawyer.

Award—a decision or result in favor of a claimant.

Bailiff—a person usually in uniform who is responsible for keeping order in the courtroom and assisting both the judge and the public.

Bar—a group of practicing lawyers.

Bench—the seat occupied by the judge in the courtroom; also may refer to the court itself.

Best evidence rule—the original document instead of a copy.

Breach—a break or change, such as a broken agreement.

Calendar call—the start of each session of court. The clerk or judge calls all of the cases that will be heard on that day.

Casualty—injury, damage, or loss.

Civil law—law dealing with disputes between individuals.

Claim—a demand for something as one's rightful due (in Small Claims Court, money).

Claimant—person bringing or filing a claim; the same as petitioner or plaintiff.

Clerk—the administrative officer who is in charge of the Small Claims Court office and who assists the public in filing claims.

Constable—a civil enforcement officer who serves legal notices and attempts to collect awards.

Contract—an agreement by two or more parties.

Counterclaim—a claim for money that a respondent may bring against a claimant in Small Claims Court.

County clerk's office—the place where all legal documents are recorded in the county; may be called office of the registrar.

Court attendant—a man or woman in uniform; usually the judge's assistant or personal attendant.

Court bond—money deposited with a court in the full amount of the judgment as security during an appeal.

Court officer—a court attendant, bailiff, or civil enforcement officer.

Court reporter—the person who records all of the words stated in court and who will transcribe them, if necessary.

Criminal law—law that when violated is prosecuted by the state.

Cross-examination—the questioning of your opponent or your opponent's witness who has made a statement in court.

Decision—a determination of the facts and a conclusion reached by the judge.

Default—failure to appear at the proper time in court, resulting in an award against the nonappearing party.

Default judgment—an award in favor of the person asking for a judgment when the opponent does not appear in court.

Defendant—a person or company against whom a claim is made.

Defense—a set of facts that would deny or modify the claim.

Demonstrative evidence—evidence furnished by tangible items in view.

De novo—all over again, as if it never occurred.

Direct case—all of the facts and proof on behalf of the person making the claim.

Direct testimony—sworn statements made in person in open court.

Dismissal—a termination of a claim either because the claimant did not appear in court or because the claimant failed to provide adequate evidence to support the claim. In the latter instance, the judge will rule, "No cause for action."

Document—any written material that in itself proves a fact, such as a receipt, a canceled check, a birth certificate, etc.

Glossary of Terms

Enforcement—the procedure used to collect an award.

Execution—an action taken by a civil enforcement officer to collect an award by liquidating the assets of the judgment debtor.

Hearsay—evidence that is not verifiable since it came from an outside source; therefore, not acceptable as proof.

Income execution—a garnishment against wages. The court orders a percentage of wages taken from the debtor's paycheck each week to satisfy a judgment or debt.

Indemnify—to pay any sums of money on behalf of another for claims brought against him or her.

Insurance—a contract binding a company to indemnify you against a specified loss in return for premiums paid.

Judgment—a decision entered upon the official record of the court.

Judgment creditor—the successful party in Small Claims Court once a judgment has been entered; a person to whom money is owed by court order.

Judgment debtor—the unsuccessful party in court; the person who, by court order, owes money to another.

Jurisdiction—the power of a court to administer justice; the extent of a court's authority.

Jury trial—a hearing in which factual issues are determined by a group of impartial people from the community.

Landlord—a person or corporation who owns property and who rents to others.

Lawsuit—a case brought in court.

Liability—legal responsibility.

Lien—a right that a creditor has over specific real or personal property of a debtor. It is recorded or filed against the property and serves as a notice to all subsequent would-be purchasers that the creditor has a prior claim on the property. A lien, in effect, inhibits the sale of the property.

Litigant—a person making a claim and/or the person against whom a claim is made.

Litigate—to bring legal action in court.

Marshal—a civil enforcement officer of the court.

Mitigation of damages—the lessening of a loss by doing certain acts; keeping your loss at a minimum.

Municipal Court—court with local jurisdiction.

Notice of claim—a notice sent to a municipality prior to filing a claim of negligence against the municipality; it must be sent within a specific number of days after the occurrence of the event.

Oath—a pledge to tell the truth.

Party—a person who brings a claim or a person against whom a claim is brought.

Personal property—a tangible item; goods; cash or other negotiable forms of currency; all property that is not real property.

Petitioner—a person asking the court to grant relief.

Physical evidence—a tangible item presented as an exhibit.

Plaintiff—a person bringing a claim.

Prima facie case—a case backed by sufficiently strong evidence that, if not questioned, results in an award.

Property execution—the taking of property to satisfy a judgment or lien; the sale of property to satisfy a debt or lien.

Pro se—representing yourself without an attorney.

Real evidence—evidence furnished by tangible items on view, as opposed to verbally presented evidence.

Real property—real estate, such as land or buildings.

Rebuttal—Statements or proof given at the time of trial by the claimant in response to the respondent's defense.

Release—an agreement not to hold another person responsible for damage.

Respondent—person or company against whom a claim is made; a defendant.

Satisfaction—a document filed to indicate that the judgment has been paid and the decision complied with.

Set-off—a defense against a claim that states an amount of money owed to the defendant and that lessens the net amount of the claim.

Sheriff—a civil or criminal enforcement officer.

Statute of limitations—a time limit within which a claim must be filed; this differs in each type of claim and in various jurisdictions.

Stenographer—the official court reporter who records in writing all of the words stated in court and who will transcribe them, if necessary.

Glossary of Terms

Subpoena—an order of the court requiring a person to appear before the court.

Summons—a notice that a case is being presented against you at a certain time and day. If you fail to appear, the person asking for an award will win by default.

Tenant—one who rents real property.

Testimony—everything stated under oath.

Witness—a person who takes an oath and testifies.

Witness stand—the chair in which the person who is testifying sits (in many Small Claims Courts, people stand before the judge).

Index

Accident reports, 21
Address of respondent, 22
Adjournment, 25
Aggravation, 16
Airlines, 191
Alimony, 52–56
Appeals, 9, 12, 33, 46–47
  notice of, 46
Arbitration Center, 19
Arbitrators, 12, 19, 33
Assault cases, 187–188
Attorney, 4–5, 11, 25, 34–35
  fee, 23
Automobile:
  accidents, 14–15, 40–41, 136–142
  insurance, 3, 40–41, 74–77, 136–139, 173
  and negligence resulting in accident, 136–142
  and negligence while performing service on, 142–144
  repair, 122–125
Award, 11, 29, 42–44
  collection of, 11, 44–46
  and interest, 29–30,

Bailments, 150
Bills, as evidence, 16, 30
Bridge district, suits against, 174

Cases. *See also* Claim
  number, 24
  preparation of, 26–27
  presentation of, 27–32
  types of, 22, 49
Charts, 27, 38
Checks, as evidence, 6, 21, 30, 38
Child support, 52–56
Children. *See* Infants
Cities, suits against, 174, 175
City court, 9, 20
Civil cases, 9
Civil courts, 9
Civil enforcement officer, 11, 45
Claims:
  defense against, 36–41
  determining amount of damage, 23

Claims (*continued*)
   documentation of, 16–17, 20, 21, 22, 26, 27, 30, 38
   filing. *See* Filing of claim
   validity of, 6, 13–19, 24
   waiting period for hearing, 10
Clerk, 16, 17, 20
   meeting with, 21–25
Collection of judgments, 11
Community Dispute Center, 19
Companies, suits against, 4
Consequential damages, 15, 23, 85, 104–108
Constable, 11, 45
Contracts, 51–64
   breach of, 51–52
   failure to fulfill, 13, 14, 57–61
   government, 176
   insurance, 65–77
   services not performed, 61–64
Corporations, suits against, 11, 22
Counterclaims, 11, 38, 119–121
   auto accidents, 138
County, suits against, 174
Court officer, 45
Courts:
   locating, 20
   types of, 9, 20
Criminal cases, 9
Crossaction, 40

Damages:
   abstract, 16
   consequential, 15, 23, 85, 104–108
   determining amount of, 23
   intentional, 184–188
   limits of, 4, 8, 9
Decision, 7, 32
   for claimant, 42–43
   no cause for action, 43
   reserved, 43–44
Default judgment, 29, 30, 45
Defense, 36–41
Dental insurance, 70
Deposits, 85
Depreciation factor, 69
Diagrams, 27, 38
Dispute Settlement Center, 19, 188
District Court, 20
Divorce decree, 52, 54, 55, 56
Documents, 16–17, 20, 21, 22, 26, 27, 30, 38
   subpoena of, 27, 145

Estimates of damage or repair, 16, 21, 27, 30
Eviction proceedings, 86
Evidence, 27, 30, 31, 38
Execution of judgment, 45

Fee schedules, 131
Felonies, 9
Filing of claim, 20–21
   fee, 5, 11, 20, 21, 23, 43
   prompt, 17
   receipt, 24

Index

Financial loss, 14–19
Financial status, 10
Fire department, suits against, 174

Geographical jurisdiction, 19–20
Goods. *See* Loaned goods, Merchandise, Missing Goods
Government, suits against, 4, 174–183

Health insurance, 70–74
Heartbreak cases, 6–7, 50. *See also* Contracts
   division of property, 163–164
   return of personal property, 160–163
Homeowners insurance, 66–69

Infants, 167–168
   actions against, 173
   actions by, 50, 167–172
Injury, intentional, 184–188
Installation, improper, 108–111
Insurance:
   auto, 3, 40–41, 74–77, 136–139, 173
   company failure to pay, 65–77
   health, 70–74
   homeowners, 66–69
Intentional damage or injury, 184–188
Interest, 29–30

Judgment:
   collection of, 11
   creditor, 140
   debtor, 140
   default, 29, 30, 45
   enforcement, 32
   execution of, 45
Judges, 7, 9, 29, 30, 31
Jury trials, 11–12
Justice of the Peace, 9
Justice of the Peace Court, 20

Landlord-Tenant claims, 78–90
   against landlords, 3, 4, 14, 79–87
   against tenants, 16, 87–90
Lawyers. *See* Attorneys
Leases, 21, 78–90
Legal language, 31, 39
Liability, 16, 18
Loaned goods, damage to, 149–150
Luggage, 191

Marshal, 11, 24, 45
Mediators, 19
Medical insurance. *See* Health insurance
Merchandise, defective, 27, 39, 91–111
   and consequential damages, 104–108
   and good faith respondent, 101–104
   improper installation, 108–111

Missing goods, 160–163, 184–194
Monetary jurisdiction, 19–20
Money due, based on promise to pay, 164–166
Municipal courts, 9, 20
Municipal suits. *See* Government, suits against

Name, legal, 21–22
Negligence, 50, 135–158
   auto accidents, 136–142
   damage to goods in possession of others, 149–158
   government, 174–176
   in performance of service, 147–149
   by workmen, 142–146
No cause for action, 43
Notice. *See* Service of notice
Notice of claim, 175, 176

Photographs, as evidence, 27, 38
Prima facie case, 29
Professional services. *See* Services and repairs performed
Promissory notes, 15, 21, 56–57
   enforcement of, 51
Property damage, 15, 16. *See also* Merchandise, Missing goods
Property division, 7, 34, 163–164

Receipts, as evidence, 6, 38
Referees, 33
Release of liability, 18
Rent, 85–86, 90
Repairs. *See* Services and repairs performed
Reserved decision, 43–44
Respondent:
   current address of, 22
   failure to appear in court, 29, 30
   good faith, 39, 101–104
   legal name of, 21–22

Satisfaction, filing, 46
School district, suits against, 174, 175
Security deposits, 3, 4, 14, 79–85
Separation agreements, 51, 52–56
Service of notice, 22, 23–24, 36, 37
Services and repairs performed, 112–134
   improper, 3–4, 15, 31–32, 39, 113–122
   improper, unnecessary, unauthorized, 122–130
   improper installation of product, 108–111

Index

negligence during. *See*
    Negligence
rendered properly but unpaid,
    4, 15, 130–134, 170–172
Settlement, prehearing, 25–26
Sewer district, suits against,
    174, 176, 177–178
Sheriff, 11, 24, 45
Small claims court:
    limits of damages, 4, 8, 9
    speed of, 5
    table of variations, listed by
        state, 97–207
Statute of limitations, 17
Stolen goods. *See* Missing goods
Subpoena, of witness, 27, 38
Subpoena duces tecum, 27, 145

Telephone call expenses, 107–108, 166

Tenant claims *See* Landlord-Tenant claims
Third-party action, 40
Town Court, 20
Towns, suits against, 174, 175
Transportation costs, 30
Tunnel district, suits against, 174

Union rates, 131

Village Court, 20
Villages, suits against, 174

Water authority, suits against, 174
Witnesses, 6, 11, 17, 26, 31
    subpoena of, 27, 38